"*The Dutiful Worrier* is an excellent self-help book. It provides extremely helpful strategies for leading a less anxious and more fulfilling life. Lucid and cleverly organized into sections that make it easy to read and understand, it draws on the thoughts and findings of outstanding clinicians and scholars. I enthusiastically endorse and recommend *The Dutiful Worrier.*"

> —Arnold A. Lazarus, PhD, ABPP, Distinguished Professor Emeritus in Clinical Psychology at Rutgers University and executive director of The Lazarus Institute in Skillman, NJ

"Worry, no matter how good the reason, is not healthy. As Albert Ellis stated, 'Worry is itself one of the most painful conditions.' Elliot Cohen shows how to use a four-step process to identify, refute, replace, and monitor well-meaning worry. I recommend you follow this four-step program and learn to concentrate on actual troubles and not the imaginary ones."

> —Jon Carlson, PsyD, EdD, Distinguished Professor in psychology and counseling at Governors State University in University Park, IL

"A unique book that gets at the meta-cognition underlying people's compulsive worry: the belief that they must keep obsessing about future possibilities so that somehow in their ruminating despair they will discover the perfect solution. In addition, Cohen's book provides one of the clearest and most succinct demonstrations I've ever seen of the four-step process for identifying and changing irrational beliefs—a great general introduction to CBT."

> —Janet L. Wolfe, PhD, former executive editor of the Albert Ellis Institute

"If you are tired of sweating things that never happen, this highly informative book is for you. Use the exceptional ideas and exercises within to free yourself from worry and to unleash a happier, more productive you. This may be the last book you'll need on defeating worry."

—William J. Knaus, EdD, author of
The Cognitive Behavioral Workbook for Anxiety
and *End Procrastination Now*

The DUTIFUL WORRIER

HOW TO STOP COMPULSIVE WORRY WITHOUT FEELING GUILTY

ELLIOT D. COHEN, PhD

NEW HARBINGER PUBLICATIONS, INC.

Distributed in Canada by Raincoast Books

Copyright © 2011 by Elliot D. Cohen
New Harbinger Publications, Inc.
5674 Shattuck Avenue
Oakland, CA 94609
www.newharbinger.com

Cover design by Amy Shoup
Text design by Michele Waters-Kermes
Acquired by Jess O'Brien
Edited by Brady Kahn

All Rights Reserved

Printed in the United States of America

Library of Congress Cataloging-in-Publication Data

Cohen, Elliot D.
  The dutiful worrier : how to stop compulsive worry without feeling guilty / Elliot D. Cohen.
      p. cm.
  Includes bibliographical references.
  ISBN 978-1-57224-897-7 (pbk.) -- ISBN 978-1-57224-898-4 (pdf ebook)
  1. Worry. 2. Obsessive-compulsive disorder--Handbooks, manuals, etc. I. Title.
  BF575.W8.C64 2011
  152.4'6--dc22

                                    2011005857

13   12   11

10   9   8   7   6   5   4   3   2   1

First printing

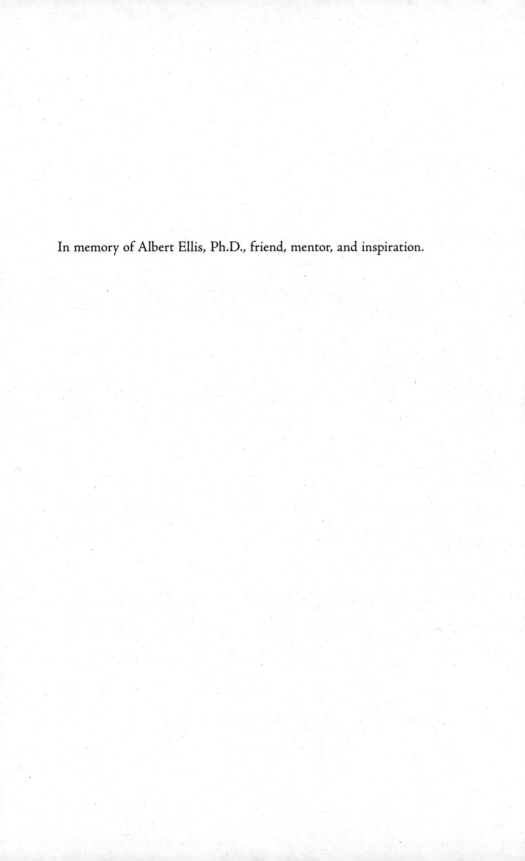

In memory of Albert Ellis, Ph.D., friend, mentor, and inspiration.

Contents

Acknowledgments

Many of the ideas in this book are based on the work of the late, great Albert Ellis, the grandfather of cognitive behavioral therapy. Since the mid-1980s, when I first began to develop the therapeutic approach embedded in this book, Al was a friend, mentor, and inspiration. In addition to teaching me the mechanics of his therapy, he read my manuscripts, shared his ideas with me, and endorsed my books. His positive influences on my life and on the ideas contained in this book are inestimable.

I would also like to thank my wife, Dr. Gale S. Cohen, a licensed mental health counselor, with whom I have discussed many of the ideas contained in this book. Having first met in high school, Gale and I have had a lifetime of collaboration, and my love, admiration, and appreciation for this beautiful woman continues to blossom.

The ideas in this book have also evolved out of my work with clients, students, and colleagues. To these individuals, collectively and individually, I also owe a debt of gratitude.

Finally, I would like to thank my editors at New Harbinger: Kayla Sussell, Jess Beebe, Jess O'Brien, and Brady Kahn. These incredibly talented professionals have provided invaluable editorial wisdom, insight, and guidance throughout the preparation of this book.

Introduction

Do you tell yourself that you must keep thinking about a perceived problem until you find a certain or nearly certain solution? Do you spend many hours of your life ruminating about these things? Do you feel guilty if you aren't worrying? Do you sometimes think that things are too good and that there must be something further to worry about? Do you tend to think that your partner, family members, or friends must also worry along with you? If so, then you may be suffering from *dutiful worrying*. This type of chronic worrying, if left untreated, can take its toll on your personal happiness. Much like a drug or alcohol addiction, it can also disrupt the lives of other people, especially those with whom you live.

Worrying is an uneasy state of consciousness about the possibility of a future unwanted event or state of affairs. The worrier perceives such negative future possibilities as being problematic, that is, as raising serious, unanswered questions: *Is my mother going to recover from her illness? Will my son ever settle down? Will I be laid off? Will I ever find a mate?* Thus, your mother might not recover, your son might not settle down, you might be laid off, and you might never find a mate.

Worrying can be focused on what to do about such problems: *What can I do to ensure that my mother gets adequate medical treatment? What can I do to help my son settle down? What can I do to avoid getting laid off? What can I do to find someone with whom I'm compatible?* Dutiful worrying is this latter sort of what-to-do-about-it worrying.

Such worrying is about unanswered questions you have, which, depending on how they're answered, can negatively impact the welfare, interests, or needs of someone or other—often your loved ones. Such concerns about the welfare, interests, or needs of other people (even your family pet) are called *moral problems*. So, in a broad sense, dutiful worrying is about solving your (perceived) moral problems. Unfortunately, dutiful worrying is a self-defeating and inadequate way of trying to solve these problems. Indeed, as this book demonstrates, part of learning how to overcome your dutiful-worrying habit includes finding a better way to address your moral problems.

Since dutiful worriers perceive that serious negative possibilities are at stake, they also feel immense pressure to prevent such negative outcomes. In fact, dutiful worriers commonly tell themselves that as long as there is something seriously wrong in their lives, they cannot allow themselves to be happy but must instead continue to ruminate and be upset until the situation is resolved. For example, a mother may not allow herself to have any peace if her child is ill. She tells herself that as long as he is suffering, she must also suffer.

The word "worry" itself is derived from the Old English *wyrgan*, which means "to strangle." The metaphor of strangulation is a fitting beginning for the modern use of the term, which signifies a troubled or uneasy state of consciousness.

All worrying is inherently negative and involves ruminating about something you perceive to be extremely bad, which is a sort of emotional self-strangulation. In this respect, worrying is always unhelpful but is unlikely to do serious damage unless it is chronic. So you might get upset if a loved one is late, and worry for a bit, only to stop worrying when he arrives home safe and sound. Although unhelpful, this sort of worrying is relatively benign as long as it does not become excessive. On the other hand, dutiful worrying tends to be chronic worrying. That is, it involves a habit of worrying, which in the long run can take its toll on your happiness.

Why It's Hard to Quit

Dutiful worrying can be distinguished from other forms of worrying and anxiety by virtue of the connection between worry and guilt. If you dutifully worry, you feel guilty when you try to stop worrying and therefore think that you have to worry. This is why such guilt-driven worry (which might also be called *guilty worrying*) is less likely to be treated than other forms of worrying. Dutiful worriers mistake it for a way of life that is not only acceptable but also morally incumbent on them. That is, you think that if you didn't worry about and try to control what might happen, you would be acting irresponsibly and therefore would be a bad person. So, although people who dutifully worry invariably experience severe, debilitating stress, they see this as the personal sacrifice they must make in order to do the right thing and be good, or at least not bad, people.

This way of thinking can dispose you to a persistent and vicious cycle of stress. There is usually something you could find wrong on which to fixate and ruminate, and when one problem is "resolved," it's not long before another problem can be perceived, and so the agonizing, painstaking worry typically continues on and on. And if someone close to you resists putting life on hold in order to give her undivided attention to the issue at hand, you may feel frustrated: "Don't you even care?"

As a result, dutiful worrying can take its toll on your interpersonal relationships, including your marriage, your relationship with your children, and your friends. People who dutifully worry typically live in pressure cookers, where a slow boil can suddenly speed up. Even when life seems relatively peaceful, there is still, for family members, the expectation that it won't last. And it usually doesn't!

Many dutiful worriers love their family members so much that they think they must worry about their welfare and that they are bad people if they don't. However, such thinking can be self-defeating. *Maybe my husband will have a heart attack unless I worry about him at all times,* you say to yourself. Indeed, one way to increase the nervous tension in the household is to make your husband the object of your worry! Such added stress is good for neither you nor your loved ones.

Why You Should Stop Worrying

If you are a dutiful worrier, please don't conclude from this that you should overcome your dutiful worrying for the sake of your loved ones. Take care not to displace your worrying onto the welfare of others. Far from addressing your dutiful worrying, you will then have found a new outlet for it and further solidified your habit!

I urge you to overcome your dutiful worrying for your own sake. The people close to you will benefit as well. But to overcome your worrying, you must first accept that you have this problem. Denial of it can be a major hurdle.

As mentioned, dutiful worrying is different from other forms of worrying, for the worrier sees his worrying as a moral duty and therefore does not immediately recognize that anything needs to change. Until you recognize and accept that your worrying is a problem, you are unlikely to ever change. That's right—not ever—because you will believe that all the anguish you have piled onto yourself and your loved ones is part of what you must do.

As you will see, dutiful (or guilty) worrying is characterized by irrational thinking. This book will show you what this pattern of thinking looks like, explain just why it's irrational, and help you to identify and overcome it in yourself. This book provides a four-step program to reduce your self-imposed stress and offers exercises and homework assignments that will help you defeat the chronic and debilitating habit of dutiful worrying.

CHAPTER 1

How Dutiful Worrying Undermines Your Happiness

If you are a dutiful worrier, then chances are you spend much of your life ruminating about problems and feeling guilty when you try to stop. In this way, dutiful worrying excludes and crowds out constructive activities. Take, for example, the case of a client named Jenna.

• Jenna's Story

Jenna was a forty-year-old working mom who confided that she was having trouble meeting her responsibilities at work and was on the verge of being fired because she found herself filling up the hours of her workday ruminating about her personal problems instead of getting her assignments done. Jenna was less concerned about losing her job than she was about these other problems.

One of her children, a fifth-grader named Tommy, was getting into fights at school with other children and had been talking back to his parents and having temper tantrums at home. While Tommy had been seeing the school psychologist for over a month, his behavior did not appear to be improving.

So Jenna sat at her desk and for hours each day ruminated about her son's problems, trying to find "the right" approach to dealing with him. For Jenna, life was a dark tunnel in which she was trapped, and it was up to her to find a way out. If she didn't, then life could not go on, at least not in any meaningful way. So, she "just had to" worry, for the sake of her family, to find a way out of this dire situation. She believed that otherwise there might be terrible consequences and she would have let her family down.

So, as she perceived it, she had a solemn duty to worry and to keep worrying until, somehow in her ruminating despair, she would discover the perfect or near-perfect solution.

Jenna did not see any way out of this dark tunnel. If she tried to stop worrying, she would incur the wrath of her guilt. This guilt would rear its ugly head in fleeting thoughts that kept her in bondage to her worry: *What kind of mother are you to abandon your own son? Don't you love your little boy enough to anguish over him? How could you live with yourself if something happened to him?*

Not only did Jenna immerse herself in worry, but she also expected her husband to do the same. As she saw it, he too had a duty to worry about their child. After all, he was Tommy's father. *How could he take his eye off the ball at a time like this when his own flesh and blood needed his help? What kind of father could do that?*

So conceived, it's no wonder that Jenna felt overwhelmed by her personal problems and was unable to concentrate at work under such stressful conditions.

Can you sympathize with how Jenna was feeling? "Oh, I understand that feeling," you might say. "I've been there before, myself. I know just how she felt." True enough, but be careful, for it is one thing to have sympathy for someone who is going through difficult times and quite another thing to say that what this person is doing about her situation (namely, worrying herself sick instead of doing her work) is rational or helpful.

Guilt and Worry

Let me be blunt. There simply is no moral duty to worry yourself into an early grave when you have problems, real or imagined. So there's really no reason to feel guilty about not worrying. That's right. I said no reason, because guilt always arises from the perception of having done something morally wrong. When someone feels guilty, she feels bad about having violated some moral principle, about having breached a duty of some kind. But when you have a problem, you do not have a moral duty to torment yourself with worry. So there is literally nothing to feel guilty about when you refuse to worry.

While there appear to be biological factors that predispose people toward worrying, dutiful worrying always involves a choice. In fact, the root of dutiful worrying lies in a moral decision. Dutiful worrying involves an earnest although self-defeating attempt to do the right thing. People who are dutiful worriers choose to worry, and do so because they perceive that worrying is a moral imperative. Thus Jenna tried to justify her worrying by claiming that her personal problems took priority over her work. But Jenna had a choice. She didn't have to worry. She could choose to do her work and keep her job. In the end, this was the choice she did, in fact, make. But before she did, the needless stress she created by worrying took its toll.

Faulty Moral Reasoning

Dutiful worrying involves self-defeating moral reasoning, or moral decision-making. As you will see, *moral decisions* are about what to do when someone's welfare, interests, or needs, (including your own) are at stake. *Self-defeating moral reasoning* is moral reasoning that backfires. It doesn't advance anyone's positive welfare, interests, or needs, but instead makes things worse.

Thus, Jenna made a moral decision when she decided to ruminate instead of doing her work. But it's not rocket science to see that Jenna's moral decision was a self-defeating one. She helped no one and just made things worse for herself and the rest of her family.

So why in the name of goodness would anyone make such a self-defeating decision? It defies rationality. But that's just it. Such moral reasoning is irrational.

When thinking is irrational, you can say it contains fallacies. A fallacy is a way of thinking or reasoning that tends to be self-defeating; that is, it has a proven track record of frustrating personal and interpersonal happiness. Dutiful worrying is chock-full of fallacies.

Confronting Your Distorted Thinking

Some people go through a lifetime not realizing that the key to their unhappiness is their distorted thinking. They rely on certain habits of thinking to make life choices, never questioning them and never realizing that these ways of thinking are irrational.

Some other people come to see that their thinking contains fallacies and that they are being irrational, yet they continue to make irrational decisions. As you will see, realizing that you are thinking irrationally is only a start; you will have to do more work to overcome the fallacies in your thinking. You may say, "I have no fallacies in my thinking." The truth is that if you are human, you are fallible. In fact, it's a fallacy to think that you are perfect and have no fallacies. Give up that fallacious idea, and you will be more likely to make progress in overcoming your fallacies. It's okay to admit that you're imperfect and the world is imperfect. It's an excellent place to start.

Three Primary Fallacies

If you are a dutiful worrier, then you definitely have fallacies in your moral reasoning. In fact, there are three primary fallacies that typically feed chronic, dutiful, worrying reasoning. These fallacies may go by different names, but let's call them *losing-control anxiety*, *self-damnation*, and *dutiful perfectionism*. This destructive threesome can lead you to worry chronically, distract you from your real duties, and destroy the quality of your interpersonal relationships.

Take a look at this reasoning: *If I don't worry about my problem, I won't be able to control what happens, and something awful might happen. Then it would be my fault and make me a bad person. So I just have to keep worrying about it.* Does this sound familiar? Does it sound like you?

Such dutiful worrying is control-centered. It arises from anxiety about being unable to control the course of future events. This self-defeating series of fallacies typically consists of two premises that piggyback on each other and lead to a perceived duty to worry, as follows:

1. "If I don't keep worrying until I'm certain that I've found the best [perfect or near-perfect] solution to my problem, I might fail to control the situation, and something awful might happen." (losing-control anxiety)

2. "Then it would be my fault for having let it happen, which would make me a bad person." (self-damnation)

3. "So I have a moral duty to keep worrying until I'm certain that I've found the best solution to my problem." (dutiful perfectionism)

Do you see how the first two thoughts lead to the conclusion? Do you see how you may try to use these two premises to build a moral case for keeping yourself in a state of agitation? First you focus on the possibility that something awful could happen if you don't figure out for sure how best to control the situation. Second, you tell yourself how you would be at fault for having let this awful thing take place and, therefore, would be a bad person. Thus, you come to the conclusion that you must keep searching until you are sure that you've come up with the perfect (or near-perfect) solution to your perceived problem. So, motivated to avoid the guilt of messing up and being a bad person, you believe you have a moral duty to solve your problem. A perfect solution (if one were possible) would be risk free. It would allow you to control the world exactly the way you want it to be. In applying such perfectionist logic, you demand certainty that your solution will work; there can be no room for slip-ups, no room for being human.

Like Atlas holding up the world, control-centered dutiful worrying demands more than what is humanly possible. It exacts its price in the failure to realize that you are but a finite being with limited powers and resources. This moral argument requires that you use yourself up and wear yourself out attempting to control things.

So if you are a dutiful worrier, then you are a perfectionist who lives in an imperfect world. How stressful!

Types of Dutiful Worriers

You may be a dutiful worrier who is not self-damning. Indeed, there is a difference between doing something wrong and being a bad person. Good people can make mistakes. The guilt you experience may result more from your perception of having done something wrong than from a perception that you are bad or unworthy. Some dutiful worriers think they must deprive themselves of happiness and make themselves suffer when something goes wrong: *If I don't keep worrying and making myself unhappy about what's wrong, then that would mean I didn't care enough about it, and then I'd be a bad person. So I have to keep worrying and making myself unhappy until the problem is resolved.*

Maybe a loved one is having a problem. Perhaps your child is being bullied at school and is distraught about it. Do you tell yourself that you just can't allow yourself to be happy as long as this matter is unresolved—that you would be a bad parent if you didn't worry? Dutiful worriers with these self-sacrificial ideas demand that the world be perfect, or near perfect, before they can stop worrying. If this describes you, you will grow old worrying (if you don't worry yourself to death sooner), because you will always find something you will perceive to be flawed enough to worry about. Fortunately, this prognosis can change if you give up your dutiful worrying.

To see just where you stand, take the following dutiful-worrying inventory.

THE DUTIFUL-WORRYING INVENTORY

Questions	Answers
1. Have you ever found yourself going over and over something, analyzing it in your mind, thinking that you have to keep thinking about it?	If yes, go to 2. If no, go to 6.
2. Have you ever thought that if you ignored this perceived problem and relaxed, that something might slip by you and something very bad might happen as a result?	If yes, go to 3. If no, go to 6.
3. Would you think yourself a bad (or unworthy) person if you didn't worry and this very bad thing really did happen?	If yes, go to 7. If no, go to 4.
4. Would you think you had done something wrong if you didn't worry and this very bad thing really did happen?	If yes, go to 8. If no, go to 5.
5. Have you ever felt guilty if you tried not to keep thinking about a problem?	If yes, go to 9. If no, go to 6.
6. Have you ever told yourself that as long as something was going wrong in your life, you had to keep ruminating and disturbing yourself over it and that you couldn't be happy until it was resolved?	If yes, go to 7. If no, go to 10.
7. You appear to have or have had the classic signs of dutiful worrying.	
8. You appear to have or have had the signs of dutiful worrying, but you may be less inclined to engage in self-damning thoughts than what is commonly true in dutiful-worrying cases.	
9. You appear to have or have had the signs of dutiful worrying, except that the basis of your guilt is indeterminate.	
10. You don't appear to have all the signs of dutiful worrying.	

• Jenna's Story (Continued)

To return to Jenna's story, these are the spectacles through which Jenna perceived the world. She told herself that if she didn't find an airtight way to help her son, his misconduct would continue to escalate and eventually he would turn to crime and end up in prison. This fiasco would be her fault for not having tried harder to help her son in his formative years. What a terrible person she would be then, and how could she live with herself now if she didn't sacrifice her happiness on the altar of chronic worry in order to foreclose such untoward future possibilities?

Jenna was indeed at her wit's end when she began therapy. What she wanted was someone to tell her what to do about her son's behavior. She was also upset that her husband didn't seem nearly as troubled about the matter as she was. She saw nothing wrong with her thinking and was surprised when she was told that her biggest problem was not the problem she was trying to solve but rather the way she was going about trying to solve it.

People who dutifully worry typically don't know they are doing it. Their moral reasoning seems impeccable to them. It's all so simple and seductive. The fallacies in Jenna's thinking seemed to her to be only common sense. Common, yes, but sense? No.

Fortunately, Jenna did come to see the errors in her thinking. And only then did she find a solution to her son's problem. When she gave up her perceived duty to upset herself, she was able to make some headway. It turned out that Jenna's dutiful worrying was a part of the problem. When Jenna stopped telling herself that she had a duty to upset herself about Tommy's behavior, she was more relaxed and Tommy was more eager to discuss things with her. As a result, rapport between the two began to improve, and Tommy's behavior began to improve.

In this book, you will have the opportunity to keep a journal as you reflect on your worrying and respond to the different exercises. The following exercise will help you begin to examine your worrying habits.

EXERCISE: Start to Look at Your Worrying

Take out a pen or pencil and answer the following questions:

1. Has worrying ever strained your relationship with a significant other, made it difficult to enjoy the company of another, relax, have fun?

2. Do you think your primary relationship might be better if you didn't worry quite as much as you do?

3. What are some of the things you worry about? Do these perceived problems seem to fall into certain categories, for example, problems with the kids, work-related problems, health-related problems?

Dutiful worriers do not necessarily worry about everything, so becoming familiar with your specific worry zones can be constructive for addressing them.

The Guilt Trap

If you are a dutiful worrier, you have unfortunately made yourself a slave to debilitating worry. This kind of slavery is perpetuated by irrational guilt arising from your perception that it is your duty to worry. In short, you continue to worry because you would feel so guilty if you didn't worry.

◆ Molly's Story

Consider Molly, a single parent who was having problems meeting men. She confided having experienced strong feelings of guilt for taking any time away from trying to increase her household income. She had told herself that she had to increase her cash flow for the sake of her child, who had special needs. So, one

Saturday night, she cancelled a date with a handsome suitor and instead stayed at home feverishly surfing the Net into the wee hours for possible financial opportunities. Not surprisingly, every opportunity she found carried too much risk and was far from ideal. The more she strained to find the answer to her prayers, the more disillusioned and frustrated she became.

Molly had wanted to go out and enjoy herself that Saturday night. She was attracted to the man who had asked her out and hoped that he would call again. Unfortunately, he never did. What kept her at home was her gnawing guilt, which stemmed from the perception that she was required to focus on solving her financial problem. It could not wait until tomorrow because by then she might have missed a critical opportunity. She just had to stay at home. Caving in to her desires would have been an act of betrayal. It would have been a selfish indulgence at the expense of providing a solution to the problem at hand. How could she look for romance at a time like this? How could she flirt? What would happen if he wanted to come back to her place? Knowing that her son was in his room asleep, trusting her with his life, how could she let him down like that? No, she was trapped, destined to be miserable and unhappy.

Indeed, for the dutiful worrier, executing the moral duty to worry can be very stressful. But notice that it is your worrying, not your circumstances, that causes you stress. You have reasoned yourself into a corner. You have chosen to believe faulty premises and have drawn the conclusion that you must worry. Moreover, you think that placing yourself and family members under such stress is what you must do to avoid feeling guilty or being a bad person. But this reasoning is flawed.

What you really need to do is to stop your dutiful worrying and free yourself from your self-imposed bondage. The next chapter discusses a four-step program for doing just that!

CHAPTER 2

Four Steps to Overcoming Dutiful Worrying

Dutiful worrying is propelled by a perfectionistic sense of moral duty—a pseudo duty—and a guilty conscience. Guilt prevents you from deviating from this pseudo duty and keeps you in a constant state of emotional stress. Accordingly, you can address your guilt by learning how to think more constructively about morality. This involves giving up your false sense of moral duty and replacing it with a sense of duty that is more rational and realistic.

This chapter introduces four basic steps toward liberating yourself from dutiful worrying: identifying the faulty reasoning that drives your worrying; refuting that faulty reasoning; replacing it with a rational perspective; and using your willpower to choose not to worry. Later chapters will cover each of these steps in more detail.

Step 1: Identify Your Faulty Reasoning

When you are in the midst of dutiful worrying, you are likely to have fleeting thoughts like the following: *How can I relax? That would be terrible. It'd be my fault. What kind of person would I be then?* These thoughts are like the pieces of a jigsaw puzzle; it may not seem clear to you how they fit together. Putting them together involves identifying the premises and conclusion of the faulty reasoning that is driving you to worry relentlessly. This would be a formidable task without an understanding of how your faulty reasoning works, but happily you have already seen in chapter 1 how your worrying usually follows a certain pattern.

A Template for Faulty Reasoning

Again, the three primary fallacies in your thinking (losing-control anxiety, self-damnation, and dutiful perfectionism) operate as the following two premises and conclusion:

1. "If I don't keep worrying until I'm certain that I've found the best (perfect or near-perfect) solution to my problem, I might fail to control the situation and something awful might happen." (losing-control anxiety)

2. "Then it would be my fault for having let it happen, which would make me a bad person." (self-damnation)

3. "So I have a moral duty to keep worrying until I'm certain that I've found the best solution to my problem." (dutiful perfectionism)

This pattern is a template you can use to identify your faulty reasoning whenever you are dutifully worrying. The three primary fallacies in this reasoning are concisely defined in the following table.

THE DUTIFUL-WORRYING FALLACIES

Fallacy	Definition
losing-control anxiety	Thinking that if you don't worry about the situation, you'll lose control of it and something awful might happen
self-damnation	Thinking you are a bad or worthless person
dutiful perfectionism	Thinking that you have a moral duty to ruminate and disturb yourself about a perceived problem until you are certain that you have found the perfect (or near-perfect) solution

Again, dutiful worrying arises out of your anxiety about not being able to control what will happen in the future. In fact, anxiety always involves apprehensiveness about the future, and the object of your worry is always a possible negative future event or state of affairs.

It is largely uncertainty about the future that fuels dutiful worrying. You commit the first fallacy when you want the future to be certain; you want a guarantee that awful things won't happen, and so you try to prevent them by worrying excessively. But, realistically, this won't work. Predictions about the future are inherently probabilistic and tentative. Ask any self-respecting meteorologist.

Why People Worry

If dutiful worrying is irrational, why do you do it in the first place? Here is a hypothesis. If you are a dutiful worrier, you are uncomfortable in a world where there is probability instead of certainty. You want to be sure that bad things won't happen, so you transmute this desire into a demand to control the future. You want yourself and the people you care about to be free and clear of poisonous insects, murder, rape, drug addiction, embezzlers, burglary, mass destruction, automobile accidents, homelessness, cancer, or whatever is your particular set of boogeymen or things that go bump in the night.

You dread these things. So you exaggerate their probabilities. Spurred on by the fear of losing control, you exaggerate the likelihood of events you fear the most and catapult them into serious prospects. You then anoint them with words like "terrible," "horrible," and "awful" and dedicate yourself to slaying these demons before they strike.

So there you are, feeling like the fate of the universe is in your hands, like Buffy the Vampire Slayer, watching at every turn for these suckers to make their move. But you must make sure that you don't screw up because, as you perceive it, the stakes are incredibly high—awful things might happen if you aren't careful and in control at all times. So you need to be on guard at every moment, making sure that you don't miss a cue. You must be perfect.

And what if you did screw up? Well, then you would be a failure, for you would have fallen asleep on duty. How then could you stand to look at yourself in the mirror?

Therefore, you must always be on guard. This is your destiny—to worry yourself into an early grave. For at least then you will not be guilty as charged.

Step 2: Refute the Fallacies in Your Thinking

But none of this thinking is remotely rational. It is a tall tale fabricated from the sludge of fallacies. Fortunately you can refute the fallacies in your reasoning. This means keying in to why losing-control anxiety, self-damnation, and dutiful perfectionism are irrational and self-defeating. For example, dutiful perfectionism always involves a demand for certainty or near certainty. However, anything we know through the senses is always subject to the possibility of disconfirmation and is never certain. Even the laws of physical science are at most highly probable. Everything else under the sun, no less predicting the future, is far less probable than such natural laws. So if you want an airtight solution to your problem, you are not going to find it this side of the heaven/earth divide, no matter how much time you spend ruminating over a perceived problem. This means that it is plainly irrational to demand certainty.

Why You Should Stop Being Afraid

Fear feeds the fires of dutiful worrying; it is a fear of slipping up, of not being able to control the outcome. But you can't control everything, no matter how much you spin your wheels, and it is self-defeating to try. Indeed, since you don't have control of everything, it makes no sense to fear losing it.

You can make reasonable efforts to control events, but this doesn't eliminate the possibility that your children might get sick, you might get rear-ended in traffic, your flight might be cancelled, your lover could turn out to be two-timing you, you could get sick on your vacation, or your new car might turn out to be a lemon. It is rational to want these things not to happen, but it is irrational to demand or require that they not happen. They may still happen, regardless of what you want. Such is reality. It is imperfect. But it can still be sublimely imperfect.

EXERCISE: Look at the Effects of Worrying on Your Conscious Life

Many people who are guilty worriers will feel guilty about not worrying, for there may always be something to worry about that they are overlooking. This is a common symptom of anxiety about losing control. Do you experience such guilt? How often? Are there times when you feel worry-free and unencumbered, or is your stream of consciousness largely taken up with worrying and worrying about not worrying? Record the answers to these questions in your journal.

Now, imagine that you very rarely worry, and compare this to your current conscious life. Assuming these two states are significantly different, make a list of the pros and cons for each way of life. Which state would you prefer? Try to be objective.

Do you ever find yourself looking for things to worry about? If so, ask yourself if there is any rational justification for doing this.

Often worriers magnify risks and then go on to catastrophize about them. "Am I going to die?" you ask, after learning that the milk you just drank expired two days ago. Well, probably not. Of course, it's not impossible, but it's very, very unlikely.

EXERCISE: Examine Your Catastrophic Thinking

Recall at least two or three experiences where you catastrophized about a possible event and worried about it taking place. Write about these experiences in your journal. In each case, what evidence did you have for thinking that the things you feared would actually happen? Did they happen? Can you see how you can be your own worst enemy by blowing things out of proportion?

Why Making Mistakes Doesn't Make You Bad

Damning yourself may sound like a natural thing to do if you mess up. *What a dumbass I am*, you think, after you send an e-mail to your boss that has a glaring typo in his first name (you called him "Blob" instead of "Bob"). *Why didn't I proofread that message before I hit the send key! I have to be the biggest loser in the world.* But it is a fallacy to think that making mistakes makes you a bad person. There is no "biggest loser in the world." That's because no human being is or can be perfect. People mess up. So you can stop telling yourself that you'd be a bad person if you failed to prevent something bad from happening because you didn't worry enough. Instead, you can tell yourself you'd be only human. Indeed, if making mistakes made you a bad person, then every last one of us would be bad.

EXERCISE: Look at Your Self-Damning Thoughts

Have you damned yourself lately? Have you damned anyone else? Make a list of the words you have used to damn yourself or others. Damning language is usually highly emotive and lacking in descriptive content. For example, calling yourself a "worthless piece of garbage" describes nothing factual about you. Be on the lookout for your use of such empty, self-defeating, demoralizing language.

If you catastrophize about not being able to control the course of future events (and then tell yourself what a loser you'd be if you let such a catastrophe happen because you failed to worry enough), then you will have made your case for having a moral duty to worry. But this case would have been made on the back of fallacious thinking that has a long-standing track record of frustrating personal and interpersonal happiness. Moral duties are not supposed to be self-defeating and destructive of human happiness. They are supposed to promote the welfare, interests, and needs of human beings.

How Being a Dutiful Worrier Stresses You

Keeping yourself in a suspended state of worrying until you've found that perfect solution helps neither you nor anyone else. First, your dutiful perfectionism can never be realized in this imperfect world. Second, such a demand for perfection works in reverse by creating counterproductive emotional stress. When you are stressed, the blood in your body goes to your brain so that you have more brainpower, right? Wrong. It goes to your gross muscles and away from your brain, thereby delivering less oxygen to your brain and making it harder for you to think efficiently. Dutiful worrying makes it harder to think.

EXERCISE: Examine Your Perceived Duty to Worry

Make a list of things that you think you have moral duties to do. That is, make a list of what you think you need to do to promote the welfare, interests, or needs of yourself and the people you care about. Now make a second list of things you believe you have a duty to worry about. Are there differences between your respective lists? What are they? Are there any similarities? What are they? Are there any general conclusions you can draw from this comparison?

The preceding exercises have given you some initial practice at refuting the fallacies in your dutiful-worrying reasoning. Chapter 4 will cover this step in greater detail.

Step 3: Take a Rational Approach

As a dutiful worrier, you see many of the defects in nature without seeing many of the good things and the larger picture of which the perceived problem is but only a part. You magnify dangers, ruminate over them, and try to control them. But you do not have to do any of this. Happily, there are more constructive things you can do. As you will see, you can apply rational antidotes to correct and overcome your irrational thinking.

You will need to replace the fallacies in your thinking with a rational, realistic perspective. Taking such a perspective means having rational goals or aspirations that keep you on the straight and narrow. First, it will take courage to face your problems instead of catastrophizing about them. Second, you will learn that, as a human being, you have value that does not depend on how useful you are to others or on how well you perform. You can thus transcend your self-damning tendency and aspire toward unconditional self-respect. And third, you can replace your dutiful perfectionism with serenity as you develop more realistic expectations about yourself and the world.

Indeed, in place of each of the respective fallacies that define dutiful worrying is a *moral virtue*, an ideal that you can use to make rational choices. The following table lists each of the fallacies and its respective moral virtue:

THE MORAL VIRTUES

Fallacy	Moral Virtue
losing-control anxiety	courage
self-damnation	unconditional self-respect
dutiful perfectionism	serenity

Courage, unconditional self-respect, and serenity take you above and beyond your dutiful-worrying fallacies. That is, they not only lead you to stop committing these fallacies, they also provide standards of what it means to live well. For example, having courage not only helps to relieve your losing-control anxiety, it also sets a standard of excellence in confronting the challenges of everyday life.

When people have such ideals to aim for, they are more likely to overcome their behavioral and emotional issues. And what's so exciting about striving for these moral virtues is that it presents a challenge. There will always be room for honing your skills, working toward attaining higher and higher reaches of human excellence. But again, this is human excellence, not that of God. It won't give you superhuman powers. What it will do, however, is set you on a clear path toward acting rationally in the face of fear, respecting yourself as a person, and having realistic expectations in this imperfect world. And that's a lot.

These virtues are *habits* in the sense that you will learn to think, feel, and act, on a regular basis, in ways that are in line with a particular virtue. You can improve on each of these habits through practice, but you can also backslide if you don't work hard. Just what are you getting yourself into when you set your sights on attaining these moral virtues? To get started, here are brief snapshots of the three virtues.

Courage

Having *courage* means being in the habit of facing adversity without under- or overestimating the danger. It means following the golden mean of being neither too afraid nor too unafraid of dangers and therefore acting according to the merits of the situation. If you are courageous, you will recognize that there are degrees of bad (as well as good) things and that terms like "terrible," "horrible," and "awful" should not be thrown around frivolously. When you act courageously, you will see that even when bad things happen, they could always be worse. Being courageous means learning from your misfortunes, using them as an opportunity for personal growth, and taking reasonable risks so you can live well. It also means rationally confronting the fact that you can't control everything.

Unconditional Self-Respect

Unconditional self-respect is self-acceptance based on an understanding and appreciation of human worth and dignity. To accept yourself unconditionally is not the same as accepting or rationalizing away your misdeeds. Instead, it means distinguishing the doer from the deed and being prepared to admit you've done something wrong without condemning yourself. If you have unconditional self-respect, you will also have unconditional respect for others. Just as you would not sink your own dignity in a degrading array of dirty names, you would avoid the same in your treatment of other people. Self-respect is accordingly a cornerstone to a healthy, functional, interpersonal relationship. Cultivating it helps you to live happily with others and with yourself.

Serenity

Serenity involves a healthy acceptance of reality. It means having a realistic understanding and appreciation of what you can and cannot expect from the world. If you possess this moral virtue, then you will accept that we all have limitations and are fallible. Thus you won't demand certainty, omniscience, or control over what's not in your power. You also will be able to accept disappointment. As a serene person, you may have great goals, aspirations, and dreams, but while you can hope, you will be realistic enough not to demand that they come true. Moreover, although you will be aware of what's wrong in your life or the world, you will also affirm what's positive in your experience and won't get bogged down in the negative.

EXERCISE: Prime Up for the Virtues

For each moral virtue described above—courage, unconditional self-respect, and serenity—describe at least one example of something that you have done or plan to do that illustrates that virtue. For example, have you shown courage by taking a calculated risk and not worrying yourself sick over your decision? Have you shown unconditional self-respect by giving yourself permission to make a mistake instead of berating yourself for it? Have you illustrated serenity by making a conscious decision to avoid trying to control something that really wasn't in your power to control, such as what others might think of you?

What do you think you might do to aspire toward becoming more courageous, unconditionally self-respectful, and serene? You may want to record your ideas in your journal.

You will have ample opportunity in later chapters to work on these virtues.

Step 4: Use Your Willpower to Stop Worrying

The final and crucial step for overcoming dutiful worrying is to exercise your willpower in line with moral virtue. This is where practice will make you better (if not perfect) at controlling your tendency to guiltily worry. Even if you know that your worrying is irrational and out of sync with what is morally virtuous, you are still likely to tend toward worrying and feeling guilty if you try to stop, for it is probably an old habit.

Here, you will have to work on changing your behavior as well as your thinking. For example, it won't be enough to tell yourself that your persistent habit of worrying is irrational. You will also have to stop yourself from worrying and to force yourself to direct your attention to more constructive activities.

You can actually feel your willpower at work when you know that what you are thinking or planning to do is irrational and you stop yourself from doing it. We have all had this sense at some points in our lives. It is perceived as a sort of internal struggle. For example, you feel like giving your boss a piece of your mind because he has not given you that raise he promised you. But you also know that your current situation would be better than being unemployed in a repressed job market. So, when you feel yourself about to open your mouth and utter the fatal words "Take this job and shove it," you hold yourself back and refrain from uttering them. This is an example of willpower. The more you practice it, the stronger your willpower muscle will get.

Your final goal will be to get yourself to stop worrying and feel no guilt about it. The four-step program described here aims at helping you attain this goal through cognitive exercises as well as a gradual regimen of behavioral assignments aimed at strengthening your willpower.

For now, you can begin to stop your worrying even if you do feel guilty. Even this is a big step.

EXERCISE: Flex Your Willpower Muscle

You can easily find ways to practice using willpower in the course of everyday life. For example, did you ever try to stop yourself cold from eating your favorite food? Try it out. You can be creative in fulfilling this assignment. Suppose you are in the nacho chip–eating mode, shoveling one chip into your mouth after another. Now stop! Close up the bag and walk away, and save yourself from shoveling another thousand grams of fat into your arteries. The key is to simply find things that you tend to do but know you shouldn't do, and stop yourself from doing them. The more you can do this, the better.

If you are like most people who dutifully worry, you will tend to be self-sacrificing. That is, you will be inclined to do things for others but neglect yourself. So as a behavioral assignment, think of something you are disinclined to do, but would like to do and then make yourself do it. Maybe you've told yourself it would be selfish to buy that expensive pair of shoes you've been eyeing for months. Force yourself to buy them anyway. Being happy is not about torturing yourself with guilty worry. Life can be fun. Go out and do something you would enjoy. Tell yourself that it's part of your anti–guilty- and dutiful-worry therapy. It is.

This chapter has given you an overview of the four steps for overcoming dutiful worrying. It's time to look at each of these steps more carefully and strengthen your ability to implement them. The next chapter will help you take the first step: to identify the faulty thinking at the root of your dutiful worrying.

CHAPTER 3

How to Identify Your Faulty Reasoning

It has been said that "the mystery of life is not a problem to be solved but a reality to be experienced" (Van der Leeuw 2003, 89). Unfortunately, this useful admonition is likely to be missed if you are a dutiful worrier. As a result, you can spend many years of your life spinning your wheels, having very little to show for it.

"But sometimes my worrying has paid off," the dutiful worrier would say. "Sometimes I have managed to figure some things out that were important." If this sounds like you, the question is whether you could have come up with the same ideas or even better ones without the worry and all the anguish it has caused. Has your chronic worrying, on balance, made your life and the lives of your friends, family, and significant others any better? I would venture to say that the honest answer is no.

So what are you going to do about it? Are you going to work hard to avoid dutiful worrying and the needless stress it is causing?

If the answer is yes, the first step is to identify the faulty reasoning that sustains your dutiful worrying. You have already seen the basic pattern: first you tell yourself how something catastrophic might happen if you don't worry; then you tell yourself how it would be your fault and what a bad person you'd be; and then you tell yourself how you must therefore worry. Again, you can use this pattern of thinking as a template to identify your own faulty thinking. But first you will need to identify the objects of your worry.

What Do Your Worry About?

When you worry, there is always something you are worrying about. This is a common feature of any emotion, not just worrying. Your emotion always refers to an object. For example, if you are angry, then you may be angry about something someone said to you.

It should be emphasized that the object of your worrying is not actually causing you to worry, as if you were on the passive receiving end of worry. Rather it is you, and not the object of your worry, that does the worrying. Recognizing this is important, because to overcome your dutiful worrying, you will need to take responsibility for deciding to worry in the first place.

It's also important to note that the objects of emotions, including those of worry, may not even exist. You might be worried that you are dying of an exotic disease even though you don't have any such disease. On the other hand, worries about nonexistent objects are still real in the sense that you are experiencing distress as a result of having these worries. Even if there is literally nothing to worry about, you may not cognitively and emotionally appreciate this fact. So you will still have to work on overcoming such worries in order to feel and do better.

Worry Chains

Objects of worry are always perceived by the worrier as negative future possibilities. For example, you might be worried about the possibility that your spouse will divorce you or that your boss will fire you. If you didn't value your marriage or your job, then you wouldn't ordinarily worry about these things. The worrier usually imagines one negative event leading to another even more negative event and so on: a series of consequences that link together as a *worry chain*. For example, you might be worried about not having enough money to pay next month's rent, and you might be worried about the latter because you think it will lead to you and your children becoming homeless and destitute.

The worrier perceives the ultimate possible consequences as catastrophic. Dutiful worriers tend to characterize these possibilities in highly charged emotive language such as "awful," "horrible," "terrible," or "the worst thing that could happen." Accordingly, you declare, "It would be awful if we all ended up out on the street with no money to eat and nowhere to sleep. I couldn't live with myself if I let such a horrible thing happen to my children!"

Now, if you are to tackle your dutiful worrying and avoid its oppressive guilt, you will need to carefully articulate your worry chains. The good news is that you can easily do this by asking yourself two basic questions: "What am I worried about?" and "Why am I worried about this?"

The first question ("What am I worried about?") calls for you to be specific about the perceived negative future possibility or possibilities about which you are worried. For example, your child is on medicine and still has chest congestion, and now you are worried about the possibility that the medicine the doctor prescribed is not working.

The second question ("Why am I worried about this?") calls for you to be specific about the consequences of the perceived negative possibility elicited by the first question, "What am I worried about?" For example, you might think that your child might have an antibiotic-resistant infection.

You can then continue to repeat the "Why am I worried about this?" question until you hit bedrock, that is, until you hit on something that you are worried about for its own sake and not because it might lead to something else. This final link in your chain will typically be something you judge to be the worst possible thing imaginable. Thus you might point to the possibility that the doctor won't be able to find an antibiotic that will work. "And why am I worried about this?" you ask yourself. "My child might end up in the hospital on a respirator!"

So here is the catastrophic worry chain you would have discovered by answering the previous series of questions:

1. "The medicine the doctor prescribed might not be working." →
2. "My child might have an antibiotic-resistant infection." → 3.
"The doctor might not be able to find an antibiotic that works."
→ 4. "My child might end up in the hospital on a respirator."

How many links you have in your worry chain will depend on what you regard as your ultimate grounds for worrying. For example, you might add another chilling link to the above chain if you were thinking that your child might also die as a result of his infection. Again, the final link in your worry chain would be something that you are worried about for its own sake (not because it leads to anything else about which you are worried); it's why you are worrying about everything else in the chain.

A worry chain, like a story, will have three main parts, or links:

1. The first link, elicited by asking, "What am I worried about?"

2. Intermediary link/s, elicited by repeatedly asking, "Why am I worried about this?"

3. Final link (basis for your worrying): the consequence you perceive as catastrophic and about which you are worried for its own sake, not because it leads to anything further

EXERCISE: Complete Your Worry Chain

Answer the following questions in your journal:

1. Are you worried about something right now? Can you think of something that you were recently very worried about? Start by asking yourself, "What am I worried about?" Remember that your answer to this question should be given in terms of a negative future possibility that you are really worried about. (If you are between worries right now, then write about an old worry.)

2. After examining your answer to the first question, ask yourself, "Why am I worried about this?" Repeat this second

question as many times as it takes you to locate the final link, or the basis for your worry. Be sure to write down all the links in the worry chain that you generate.

Look at the results. You will be using this worry chain in later exercises, so keep it handy.

Identifying Your Dutiful-Worrying Reasoning

Once you know how to generate your worry chains, identifying your dutiful-worrying reasoning is a piece of cake. You have already seen how this reasoning operates as two premises and a conclusion (see chapter 2). The following template for identifying your dutiful-worrying reasoning leaves blank spaces as placeholders for the first and last links in your worry chain.

1. "If I don't keep worrying about [insert first link here]. I won't be able to control things and [insert last link here] might happen."

2. "Then I'd be a bad person for having let [insert last link here] happen."

3. "So, I have to keep worrying about [insert first link here] until I'm certain I've found the best solution to it."

To return to an example from earlier, suppose your worry chain was "The medicine the doctor prescribed might not work. my child might have an antibiotic-resistant infection, the doctor might not be able to find an antibiotic that works, my child might end up in a hospital on a respirator, my child might die." To identify your dutiful-worrying reasoning, you would fill in the blanks with the information from the first and last links of your worry chain as illustrated below:

1. "If I don't keep worrying about <u>whether my child's medicine might not work</u>, I won't be able to control things and <u>my child might die</u>."

2. "Then I'd be a bad person for having let <u>my child die</u>."

3. "So, I have to keep worrying about <u>whether his medicine is working</u> until I'm certain I've found the best solution to it."

By now, you should be able to see how dutiful-worrying reasoning operates. There are, in effect, two thought processes going on at once. The first is the worry chain itself, which involves a chain of events that you believe can lead to something catastrophic. The second thought process concerns your duty to prevent this chain of events. You conclude by telling yourself that it is your duty to worry until you are certain you've found a way to stop your worry chain from materializing.

Clearly, the key to identifying your dutiful-worrying reasoning is being able to formulate your worry chain. Usually, worriers don't have a fully articulated worry chain in mind. Rather they have only vague, fleeting, disorganized thoughts such as "We don't have enough money," "This is terrible," "What's gonna happen?" and so on. But if you take the time to systematically flesh out your entire worry chain in the manner described in this chapter, you will be in a position to carefully examine it to see if its links are realistic. As mentioned, sometimes you might be worried about nothing, but you may not realize this until you have spelled out exactly what it is you are worried about.

Most people also don't have a clear idea of the structure of their dutiful-worrying reasoning, let alone of how it relates to what they are worried about. But with your handy template for identifying your dutiful-worrying reasoning, it's easy to see. Give it a try in the following exercise.

EXERCISE: Identify Your Faulty Reasoning

Copy the template for identifying your dutiful-worrying reasoning, and fill in the blanks with the first and last links in the worry chain you constructed earlier in this chapter. Then read your dutiful-worrying reasoning quietly to yourself.

Now ask yourself if the two premises and the conclusion of this reasoning ring true to you. That is, have you been telling yourself that unless you keep worrying about this worry chain, you'll lose control and the chain of events might happen? That it would then be your fault and you would be a bad person? So therefore you have to keep worrying about it until you're certain that you've found the best (perfect or near-perfect) solution? If your answer to any of these questions is yes, then you have successfully identified an instance of dutiful-worrying reasoning that is making (or has made) your life unnecessarily stressed.

Repeat this exercise with at least one more worry chain that you have constructed. The more practice you get in identifying your dutiful-worrying reasoning, the better.

Congratulations for completing step 1 of the four-step program for overcoming your dutiful worrying. Now that you know how to identify your dutiful-worrying reasoning, the next step is to uncover its logical fallacies. The next chapter will show you how to find and refute the fallacies imbedded in this kind of reasoning. In practical terms, this means showing how dutiful worrying needlessly frustrates your personal and interpersonal happiness.

CHAPTER 4

How to Find and Refute Your Reasoning Fallacies

This chapter will help you learn to refute the reasoning fallacies that keep you enmeshed in dutiful worrying. This means proving that they are irrational and self-defeating beliefs.

Again, whenever you worry, there is something you are worried about. This is the object of your worrying. Chapter 3 showed how such objects form worry chains, which you can make explicit by first asking the question "What am I worried about?" and then repeatedly asking the question "Why am I worried about this?" until you reach something you are worried about for its own sake.

Chapter 3 also showed you how to identify your dutiful-worrying reasoning. You are now ready to look more carefully at the two premises and the conclusion of your dutiful-worrying reasoning and show exactly why they are irrational.

Why You Need to Take This Step

You might be wondering why you need to refute the fallacies in your thinking. Why not focus immediately on learning how to think differently? The answer is that by seeing exactly why these ideas are irrational, you will be more inclined to give them up. In fact, the trouble with fallacies is that they are so seductive. They have an allure that is deceptive. For example, thinking that you have to worry whenever something bad might happen may seem reasonable enough, especially if you've been doing it all your life, but this is far from the case. Instead, such a belief defeats the point of worrying.

How so? You worry because you want to control things. Your goal is to head off the bad things and, in the end, improve your life and the lives of others close to you. But what really happens when you devote your life to worrying is that you, as well as those you care about, suffer needless anguish. This makes things worse, not better. So, in trying to improve matters, you make them worse. Thus, worrying is irrational and self-defeating. Yet, like you, many well-meaning and caring people worry on a daily basis. Fortunately, to your credit, you are reading and working through the exercises in this book and are hopefully beginning to realize that there can be a brighter, more productive way of living than spending days, weeks, years, and even a lifetime, worrying.

You can begin to overcome your habit of worrying by refuting the first premise of your dutiful-worrying reasoning.

Refuting Losing-Control Anxiety

"If I don't worry about my worst fear, then I won't be able to do anything to prevent it from happening," you say. A logical premise, isn't it? Or is it?

Notice that you are assuming something in the first place, namely that there is a significant risk of a catastrophe, and also that what you are trying to stop would indeed be as bad as you think it would be. So really two questions arise: Is there a significant risk of what you are worrying about happening? And would what you are worrying about be the catastrophe you imagine?

Often, dutiful worriers magnify the risks of things happening, which keeps them in a state of anxiety about the possibility of something awful happening.

• Ashley's Story

Consider the case of Ashley, a sensitive, kind-hearted young woman who recounted her emotional upheaval and anxiety about finding someone new after her boyfriend of two years broke off their relationship. Ashley believed that she had to keep herself in a suspended state of worrying and rumination about her situation.

"So what are you worried about?" I asked.

"I'm thirty-four years old," said Ashley in an apologetic tone. "I'll probably never find another guy to share my life with."

"And why are you worried about that, Ashley?"

"Why?" she protested. "I'll be alone the rest of my life!"

Understandably Ashley was frustrated. She had thought she'd found Mr. Right and had been expecting an engagement ring. Instead, he had found someone else. This is an old story in the annals of dating history, and a common thread of thinking runs through such cases. This thinking involves a doomsday outlook, a tendency of those who've been disappointed to see the future through a pair of dark lenses. Amid the uncertainty, even a small possibility of something playing out unfavorably is exaggerated and thought to be probable.

"I'll probably never find another guy to share my life with," said Ashley. But just where does this prediction come from? From statistics about the success ratio of those who have rebounded? No. From the laws of nature? Of course not! From any other rational calculation? No. From the wounded heart? Yes!

Often, when people catastrophize, they magnify the probabilities of what they want to avoid. However, probabilities depend on facts, not on subjective preferences or a fear of negative consequences. The greater the number of eligible guys Ashley met, the greater the probability that she would eventually find a match. By meeting more men, she would increase the number of ways in which the favored outcome could happen. And this is as true at thirty-four years old as it is at twenty-one or any other stage of life: for men as well as women and for gays as well as straights. On the other hand, by catastrophizing about the possibility of finding no one, Ashley succeeded only in needlessly upsetting herself without increasing the probability of meeting anyone.

But even if Ashley did not in the end manage to find a mate, would life really be so bad? "What are you telling yourself about not finding someone else?" I asked. Ashley responded, "It would be awful! I'd go insane if I had to be single for the rest of my life."

But just what did Ashley mean by saying it would be "awful"? In a popular sense, this word (along with equivalent expressions like "horrible" and "terrible") means the worst thing possible. So perhaps she meant to say that never finding another would be the worst thing that could ever happen.

Notice, however, that the idea that nothing could be worse is unrealistic. For example, to show that things could always get even worse, psychologist Albert Ellis used the example of being tortured slowly; thus you could be tortured even more slowly (Ellis 1999).

Realistically, there are much worse fates than never finding a mate. "What about dying slowly and painfully of a fatal disease?" I asked Ashley. "Isn't that much worse?" I explained that no matter how bad something may be, there could always be something even worse. So it's always unrealistic to think things are awful in an absolute sense. "Well, maybe it wouldn't be the worst thing in the world, but it would still be awful," she quipped.

Indeed, anyone can empathize with Ashley who has been through such an experience—the unbelievable disappointment ("Is this really happening to me?"); the emotional pain; the inertia against letting go and moving on; and the sense of futility in repeating a phase of life you thought was behind you.

Ashley was also correct in saying that something extremely bad could still be awful even if some things could be worse. But there are nevertheless many things that are much worse than remaining single. What to include on a list of such relatively awful things might be subject to debate, but some reasonable candidates would be devastating earthquakes, tsunamis, and other natural disasters, mass murder, gang rape, child abduction, the Holocaust, as well as dying of a painful, terminal disease.

Did Ashley's loss even come close to any of these relatively awful things? Clearly, it did not. Even if she never were to find a mate, Ashley was overrating just how undesirable such a fate truly would be. Thus she was still alive and healthy and could look forward to new and interesting life experiences and challenges. She had good friends and a job she liked, and had intended to go back to school for a graduate degree.

In the end, Ashley came to see that her worrying about her situation was unrealistic. Seen in the light of much worse things, her situation was not, after all, awful in any meaningful sense. Neither was her fear of ending up forever single really probable, given her strong desire and motivation to meet someone, a broad circle of friends and associates, social outlets, and the availability of online dating services. There simply was no need for Ashley to worry and ruminate on the subject.

In fact, what Ashley wanted was total control over her situation. The tentative nature of the future was a major source of her anxiety. If she couldn't be sure that she would find a suitable mate, then she would not allow herself to relax and be happy. However, her demand to control the future with absolute certainty was unrealistic. The future is not something anyone can have such control over.

Neither would a world in which we could determine in advance everything, or even just the things we strongly want, necessarily be a desirable world. Indeed, it would be a rather dull one—no surprises, no challenges, nothing to get excited about. So Ashley's inability to preordain the future might have paradoxically been a reason for her to enjoy life rather than to despair over her situation.

Are you anything like Ashley? Do you feel such a sense of hopelessness, bleakly thinking that you have to keep yourself worrying and unhappy about the prospects of a dismal future? Do you experience anxiety about your inability to control the future? Do you wish that this tremendous burden could be lifted from your shoulders?

Well, it can, because you have the power to lift it. The situation is not desperate. It's you who are desperate, but you don't have to be. You can decide to stop anguishing. You can begin to do this by taking the initiative to fill out your worry chain and examine it to see if you are doing any of the following: magnifying risks, exaggerating how bad your situation is, or demanding that you control something not in your power to control. As you have seen, each of these three ways of thinking is irrational. Therefore, if you can show that your losing-control anxiety is based on any of them, you will have proven that it too is irrational.

EXERCISE: Refute Your Losing-Control Anxiety

Think of something major that you are now very worried about or have been worried about in the past. Now, build your worry chain, link by link. First ask yourself what you are worried about. Then ask yourself why you are worried about this. Each time you come up with a new worry, keep asking yourself this same question. You will know when to stop when you find something that you are worried about for its own sake. For example, "I'm worried about not having enough time to finish my exam because I might fail the exam; and I'm worried about that because I might fail the course; and I'm worried about that because I won't get my degree; and I'm worried about that because I might end up never amounting to anything; and I'm worried about that just because I'm worried about it."

Now, examine your worry chain and use the following checklist to see if you are doing any of the following irrational things:

- ☐ You are magnifying risks.

- ☐ You are exaggerating just how bad your situation really is relative to much worse things.

- ☐ You are demanding that you control something that is not in your power to control.

Did you check off one or more items? If so, you have proven the irrationality of your worry chain and refuted the first premise of your dutiful-worrying reasoning: "If I don't keep worrying about it, I won't be able to control things and it might happen."

Following the directions of this exercise, see if you can construct a few more worry chains and prove their irrationality by using your checklist. The more you practice doing this, the better you will get at it.

Refuting Self-Damnation

"If I don't find someone, that will mean I'm a failure." These were Ashley's words. She thought she had to prove her worthiness as a woman and as a human being by finding someone who wanted her. As she perceived the situation, her personal worth was on trial and, if found wanting, she would be damned.

Have you ever questioned your worth as a human being? Have you ever set the price of overcoming a life obstacle at your dignity and personal value? This is just what dutiful and guilty worriers regularly do. How much self-inflicted pressure and pain has this cost you?

• Ashley's Story Continued

"Do you know anyone you admire who is single?" I asked Ashley.

"Yes, I do," she said without pausing. "My aunt never married, but she is a wonderful human being and a very successful editor. She once had an affair, but it didn't work out. "

"So this person whom you admire is not a failure?"

"No. I've admired her since I was a little girl."

"Then why would *you* be a failure if you remained single?"

Here was a refutation of Ashley's premise that she would be a failure if she were unable to find a mate. I pointed out that she was using a double standard in rating herself as worthless while admiring her single aunt. "I never thought of it that way," she said.

And here's another refutation of self-damnation you can add to your toolbox: What's true of the part is not necessarily true of the whole. So, even if you fail at something, this doesn't mean *you* are a failure. There is a difference between the deed and the doer. If failing at something meant that the doer of the deed was also a failure, then we'd all be failures, for no one can honestly boast of never having failed at anything.

So it is not only irrational but also absurd to think that failing at something also makes you a failure. Keep this distinction between doer and deed in mind, and you can save yourself from the self-inflicted indignity of seeing yourself as a bad or worthless person whenever you fail at something or make a mistake. You are not a screwup even if you sometimes screw up. You are a human being. No need to apologize or feel guilty about that.

In fact, there are three commonplace ways of thinking that can lead you to devalue and damn yourself. First, you might have double standards by which you rate yourself as totally worthless while inconsistently rating others as worthy people. This was the case with Ashley, who berated herself for not finding a mate while continuing to admire her aunt who was also single. Second, you might confuse the deed with the doer and equate the worthlessness or wrongfulness of something you did (or failed to do) with your own personal worth or dignity. Third, you might demand perfection of yourself as a condition of your own worthiness.

These ways of thinking are all irrational ways to determine your own personal worth or dignity. Therefore, if you can show that your self-damnation is based on double standards, confusing the deed with the doer, or demanding that you be perfect as a condition of your worthiness, then you will have proven that your self-damnation is also irrational. The next exercise will show you how to do this.

In the previous exercise, you generated and refuted some of your worry chains and your losing-control anxiety. In this next exercise, you can refute the second premise of your dutiful-worrying reasoning: that you'd be a bad (or worthless) person if you let your worry chains happen.

EXERCISE: Refute Your Self-Damning Thoughts

Examine your self-damning thoughts and use the following checklist to see if you are doing any of the following irrational things:

☐ You have adopted a double standard by being harder on yourself than you'd be on other people (rating yourself as bad, worthless, or a failure and not holding others to the same standard).

☐ You are telling yourself that if you're not perfect, then you're worthless.

☐ You're confusing the deed with the doer by rating yourself rather than your deed.

If you identified one or more of these three ways of thinking, then you have successfully refuted the self-damning thoughts that can keep you worrying and feeling guilty when you try not to worry. This is because these ways of thinking are irrational and lead to irrational conclusions about your own self-worth or dignity.

Repeat this exercise at least once (the more often you do it, the better), using any other worry chains that you have generated.

Refuting Dutiful Perfectionism

Dutiful worriers tell themselves that they have to keep worrying about their worry chains until they find the best (meaning perfect or near-perfect) solution to it. Like other dutiful worriers, Ashley did this too.

• Ashley's Story Continued

"I have to keep worrying about it," Ashley told me when I asked her why she wouldn't allow herself to stop worrying. "I feel like such a loser, and then I start to feel guilty, like I should be thinking about this. It's always there in the back of my mind—'You're such a loser'—even when I'm doing something at work; and I stay up at night thinking about it, sometimes for hours.

"I signed up for online dating services. I keep checking, but all these guys are weird or there's something else wrong with them." Some, she said, were smokers; some were too fat; some too short; some too tall; some too young; some too old; some bald; some were sleazy; some nerds; some were too religious; some not religious enough; some were not smart enough; some were self-centered; some were too polite. "I'll never find anyone like my ex-boyfriend again," she declared.

Here was Ashley's tall order. Find someone perfect. And if she couldn't find such a god among men, then keep herself in a perpetual state of grief over her failure to find the ideal person. Then tell herself how awful, horrible, and terrible it would be if she couldn't find someone and what a big loser she would be.

In fact, Ashley's boyfriend was not perfect either. He too was human. And, as it turned out, he had been unfaithful for the last six months of their relationship. Nevertheless, Ashley had cast a halo over him, and no one else could measure up. He was "perfect," so none of the other guys even had a chance.

At least, not until Ashley stopped demanding perfection. "Let yourself be human, and let everyone else be human too," I said. "Give yourself permission to live in an imperfect universe." This is a world inhabited by imperfect human beings, not gods; a world that is inherently uncertain; a world in which not everything can be controlled; a world in which mistakes are part of the fabric of the universe; a world in which there is injustice.

But this is also a world in which there are plenty of opportunities for enjoyment, finding romance, and having companionship. You can attain these positive things only if you stop dutifully demanding perfection and give yourself a chance. You can attain them only if you realize that what you want or prefer is not necessarily what is or can be.

Yes, you would prefer that bad things never happen, especially to the ones you love; yes, you want to be able to control things that are dangerous or threatening. But what you prefer or want is not always what can be. So the inference from "I want (or prefer) this" to "This must be" is a fallacy. Instead of making this leap into the abyss of unreality, and ending up frustrated and disillusioned with reality, stick to your preferences: "Yes, I prefer that life not be such a hassle, but that does not mean that it must be the way I prefer it to be."

Once you give up your unrealistic demand for perfection, your perceived duty to worry will evaporate. For the duty to worry is the duty to demand that reality be just the way you want it to be: perfect. Does that mean you are without any responsibility? No! But your responsibility is not any different from any other human being's, which is to make a reasonable and realistic effort to solve your perceived problems.

In Ashley's case, this meant telling herself the following: *Yes, there is a risk that I won't find another guy to spend my life with. That is a possibility. But that doesn't mean I have to control the future. I don't have to stop living as I wait to finally get what I want. Because what I want is not what must be. I can make a reasonable effort to increase the chances that I will meet someone, and then what will be will be.*

And this is just what Ashley finally decided to do. The last time I talked to her, she was dating a man she had met at a party; he was shorter than she was and a bit overweight but lots of fun, had a thriving medical practice, and was head over heels in love with her. And he was, she said, "good in bed."

Ashley's story had a happy ending. But, as you can see, her happiness was not attained by getting everything she would have preferred. Ashley wanted an Adonis, but the man she found was no Adonis. That's because Adonis was a mythical Greek and not a real guy. Once you take off your perfectionistic spectacles, the world opens up to new and exciting possibilities otherwise missed or dismissed.

So, there are three commonplace perfectionistic ways of thinking about the world. First, you might demand certainty where there can be only possibility. Second, you might conclude that, because you want or prefer something, it must be that way. Third, you might demand perfection from an imperfect human being such as yourself.

Do you think in any of these three ways when you are dutifully worrying? Are they the basis for your dutiful perfectionism (when you tell yourself that you have a moral duty to keep worrying until you're certain that you've found the best solution to a problem)? Given that these three ways of thinking are irrational, you can prove that your dutiful perfectionism is irrational if you can show that it's based on any of them. The next exercise will show you how to do this.

EXERCISE: Refute Your Dutiful Perfectionism

Take one of your worry chains and use the following checklist for refuting your dutiful perfectionism to see if you are making irrational perfectionistic assumptions.

- ☐ You are demanding that you be certain about what to do before deciding to do it.

- ☐ You are assuming that because you want or prefer something, it must be that way.

- ☐ You are demanding more than what you can reasonably expect from an imperfect human being such as yourself.

Did you check off even one item on this checklist? If so, then you have successfully refuted the perfectionism that keeps you dutifully worrying.

Repeat this exercise at least once more (the more times, the better) with another worry chain.

You should now know how to identify the reasoning that sustains your dutiful worrying and how to refute the fallacies in this reasoning. I urge you to continue practicing these two major steps in overcoming dutiful worrying. When you start to worry about something and tell yourself you must worry about it, take the time to fill out all the links in your worry chain, plug it into the template for identifying your dutiful-worrying reasoning, and refute each of the fallacies in your reasoning by using the three checklists introduced in this chapter for refuting losing-control anxiety, self-damnation, and dutiful perfectionism. With practice, these skills can become second nature!

The next step will be to find reasonable antidotes to your fallacies. This will allow you to replace your dutiful worrying with constructive and self-fulfilling thinking.

CHAPTER 5

Taking a Rational Approach

By now you have completed the first two steps in overcoming dutiful worrying: you have identified your faulty reasoning and you have refuted the fallacies in your thinking. The next step is to replace your dutiful worrying with a sense of duty that is more rational and realistic.

Dutiful worriers tend to feel guilty anytime they try to stop worrying, but this guilt is driven by a false sense of moral duty. This chapter will show you how to think more constructively about morality. It will show you how to cultivate certain moral virtues as aspirations or goals, which will help you overcome your dutiful worrying and become less anxious and more self-confident, realistic, and productive.

To sum up, here is a table that lists the dutiful-reasoning fallacies, their definitions, their modes of refutation, and the moral virtues that you will want to cultivate:

FALLACIES, REFUTATIONS, AND MORAL VIRTUES

Fallacy	Definition	Refutation	Moral Virtue
losing-control anxiety	Thinking that if you don't worry about it, you'll lose control of the situation and something awful might happen	You magnify risks. You exaggerate just how bad your situation really is relative to much worse things. You demand that you control something that is not in your power to control.	courage
self-damnation	Thinking yourself to be a bad or worthless person	You have double standards, rating yourself as bad (worthless or a failure) but not applying the same standards to everyone else. You confuse the deed with the doer by rating yourself rather than your deed. You tell yourself that if you're not perfect, then you're worthless.	unconditional self-respect
dutiful perfectionism	Thinking that you have a moral duty to ruminate and disturb yourself about a perceived problem until you are certain that you have found the perfect (or near-perfect) solution	You demand that you be certain in a world in which you can't have certainty. You assume that because you want or prefer something, it must be that way. You demand more than what you can reasonably expect from an imperfect human being such as yourself.	serenity

Each of these moral virtues can be said to override or counteract a corresponding dutiful-worrying fallacy. So, if you have courage, you will be disinclined toward losing-control anxiety. If you have unconditional self-respect, you will be disinclined to damn yourself. If you are serene, you will be disinclined toward dutiful perfectionism. This is because these positive habits of thinking, feeling, and acting are incompatible with dutiful-worrying.

How to Cultivate the Moral Virtues

So what can you do to cultivate these moral virtues? Here is where you will need to work on changing your behavior as well as the way you think. The ancient Greek philosopher Aristotle said that people become virtuous by repeatedly acting in a virtuous manner. Any single act does not make a person virtuous. For example, telling the truth once does not make you truthful. Likewise, one courageous act does not make a person courageous. In order to acquire a virtue, you will need to cultivate a tendency toward the virtuous conduct through practice.

Furthermore, practicing moral virtue means believing in what you are doing. That is, you don't act courageously if your act is accidental. Courage involves acting according to what you think is right. It involves resolve and conviction. Overcoming your dutiful worrying will take such resolve and conviction to do what you think is right—for yourself as well as for those whom you love.

Practicing Moderation

According to Aristotle (1941), moral virtue is the golden mean that lies midway between the extremes of excess and deficiency. Therefore, being courageous entails being neither too afraid nor too unafraid. Unconditional self-respect is the mean between self-abasement and vanity or conceit. Serenity is the mean between perfectionism, on the one hand, and indifference, on the other.

Hence the key to cultivating and strengthening your moral virtues is to seek moderation. As a dutiful worrier, you tend to do the opposite of practicing moderation, but you can learn how to overcome some of your extreme, self-defeating habits and become more moderate and constructive. Cultivating moral virtue portends greater happiness and less stress in your life.

This is not to say that you are lacking in moral virtue at the outset. People can be morally virtuous in some ways while not in others. For example, dutiful worriers are often courageous when it comes to protecting family members against imminent danger. Accordingly, the goal here is to strengthen and expand the scope of your virtuosness so that you can overcome your dutiful worrying.

The following table shows how each moral virtue is a mean between the extremes of excess and deficiency:

THE MORAL VIRTUES AS GOLDEN MEANS

Excess	Moral Virtue	Deficiency
too afraid	courage	not afraid enough
vanity	unconditional self-respect	self-abasement
demanding perfection	serenity	indifference to how things are

Each moral virtue observes a middle ground between excess and deficiency. Observing this middle ground is as important in thinking as it is in, say, eating. We all know that overeating is bad for us, and so too is undereating. But what you might not know is that the same goes for your thinking. Faulty thinking involves extreme thinking much as bad eating habits involve extreme eating, and the virtues for overcoming both observe the golden mean. Thus, when people eat well, neither over- nor underindulging, we say that they have good eating habits and are temperate. And when people think well and avoid faulty thinking, we call them rational.

Every reasoning fallacy involves excess or deficiency. Thus, losing-control anxiety magnifies risks and exaggerates things by calling them awful. Self-damnation underrates you and therefore involves a deficiency. Dutiful perfectionism demands perfection in an imperfect world and therefore is excessive. The moral virtues, in opposition to these fallacies, provide the means between excess and deficiency and are therefore rational.

EXERCISE: Assess Your Tendencies to Go to Extremes

Make a list of things that you think you overdo, a list of things that you think you underdo, and a list of things you think you do in moderation. Your lists can include eating, consuming alcoholic beverages, working, cleaning, playing, socializing, or any other type of human activity. What generalizations about yourself, if any, do you think you can draw from your lists? For example, do you tend to go to extremes or observe moderation? Do you think you display the same tendencies in your thinking as you do in other aspects of your life?

Finding the Golden Mean

So how do you find the desirable mean between two extremes? How do you avoid going to extremes? Here's an analogy. Suppose you have a sweet tooth. How do you avoid overdoing sweets? Well, if you buy sweets and bring them home, chances are you're going to eat them. On the other hand, if you don't bring sweets into your house, you may eat less of them. For example, I love cheesecake, the real stuff, not the light dietetic kind but the kind with all the fat. I know that it's not healthy to eat too much of it, yet I have no problem with eating it on occasion. So my challenge has been how to identify the occasions on which it's okay for me to eat cheesecake.

Here is what I've come up with. I will not buy cheesecake at a bakery or supermarket, because I know that if I bring it home, I will end up eating more than I really should. Nor will I order cheesecake at a restaurant. However, I've made it a rule to eat my share when it's served at banquets, weddings, or other catered affairs. As a result, I find myself eating cheesecake on an average of three or four times a year without experiencing any guilt over it.

Is this arrangement completely satisfactory? Well, sometimes I'm served a piece of cheesecake that is arguably not worth eating, and sometimes the piece is utterly too small to satisfy. But, on balance, cheesecake is still in my life, and I look forward to, savor, and enjoy some now and then. Is mine a perfect system? Of course it's not, for this is an imperfect world, and I'm therefore not about to demand that I always get exactly what I want when I want it.

Notice too that it takes willpower to stay on task. I do sometimes find myself gazing at cheesecakes in the bakery section of my local supermarket, but I usually walk away empty-handed. In other words, it's not enough to have a plan; you also have to exercise willpower to stick to it. This is why the fourth step of the program for overcoming dutiful worrying is so important, because you also need to act on your plan.

As you can see from this example, having a rule or guideline at your disposal can help you to control your desires so that you avoid going to extremes. Finding and applying such rules or guidelines can sometimes make the difference between attaining or not attaining your life goals. Take, for example, what is often called *assertiveness training*, or learning how to be assertive. Being assertive is the golden mean between being timid or shy and being aggressive. The timid or shy person is understated and tends to be afraid to speak up for, or do, what she wants or thinks is right. At the other extreme is the aggressive or hostile person who goes beyond what is reasonable or just, in order to get what he wants. While the timid person tends to fall short of attaining what she wants, the aggressive person often pays the price for his aggression, which could be anything from losing the cooperation of others to spending time in prison. So how do you know when you are being assertive and not going to one of these two extremes?

Suppose you are shy and afraid to speak up in a classroom or work environment. "What if I say something and I turn out to be wrong?" you ask yourself, and then you feel your heart pounding as you imagine yourself speaking up. I well know what this feels like, because I have been there emotionally. As a high school student, I was afraid to speak up in class, but once I was in college, it became more apparent to me that some of the most outspoken individuals often had less to add to the discussion than I did. I once listened attentively to one student who dominated the class discussion. He used very large words, and the other students were very impressed. But the more I listened to this student, the more evident it became that he had nothing of substance to say, although he said it very eloquently. This experience was eye opening. If this student could dominate a classroom without having anything of substance to say, then why shouldn't I speak up when I thought that I did indeed have something constructive to say? So I formulated this rule to deal with my shyness: *Whenever I think that I have something that might be useful to add to the discussion, I should speak up.* Putting my new rule into practice wasn't easy. I would tremble inside and could feel my heart pound, but I would still force myself to speak. This took willpower, and I had to work on my thinking, too: *So what if I say something that isn't a gem of wisdom! I don't have to be perfect. No one else is.*

EXERCISE: Find a Mean to Your Extreme

Choose something from one of the lists you generated in the last exercise of things you overdo or underdo, and construct a rule or guideline to help you get closer to the mean between over- and underdoing the activity in question. Put your rule or guideline into practice starting with the next time you want to engage in the given activity.

Constructing Rational Antidotes

Avoiding extreme thinking, in particular the fallacies of dutiful worrying, is not unlike avoiding extreme eating or the extremes of aggression or shyness or any other extreme behavior. This too will involve rules or guidelines and the willpower to follow them.

So how do you avoid extreme thinking and cultivate virtuous-thinking habits? This can be accomplished by learning how to apply *rational antidotes* to your fallacies, which you can think of as rules or guidelines for attaining virtues. If you work hard at applying these rational antidotes, you can strengthen your moral virtues and weaken your tendency to engage in the fallacies that feed dutiful worrying.

There are two broad types of antidotes: *cognitive* and *behavioral*. Cognitive antidotes are ways to *reframe*, or restructure, your thinking to overcome your fallacies and become more virtuous. Behavioral antidotes are ways to act differently to overcome your fallacies and become more virtuous. As you will see, cognitive and behavioral antidotes can work together in reaching these goals.

Cognitive Antidotes

Cognitive reframing can be a powerful means for reducing your worrying, especially when used in conjunction with behavioral antidotes. Cognitive reframing involves changing the way you think about something. Concentration camp survivor Viktor Frankl provides a poignant example of cognitive reframing in his book *Man's Search for Meaning* (1984, 57):

> I looked at the sky, where the stars were fading and the pink light of the morning was beginning to spread behind a dark bank of clouds. But my mind clung to my wife's image, imagining it with an uncanny acuteness. I heard her answering me, saw her smile, her frank and encouraging look. Real or not, her look was then more luminous than the sun, which was beginning to rise.

Under the oppressive and subhuman conditions of a Nazi concentration camp, Frankl was still able to find momentary meaning in life in the contemplation of the mutual love between his wife and himself, even though she was probably already dead. This was not a retreat from the bleak truth, because Frankl acknowledged the desolation of his circumstances; nor was it delusional, since he made no assumption that it was real. Yet, for a brief moment, he was able to find bliss through such a cognitive restructuring.

It is unlikely that your situation is anywhere near the magnitude of dehumanization that Frankl endured, yet his experience shows how it's possible to constructively reframe almost any situation. And this is precisely the point. It is within your power to avoid your chronic stream of worries by taking a different perspective.

Have you had a spat with your significant other? Well maybe you can sit down and have that long overdue heart-to-heart. Did you have a fender bender? Well, it's a good thing no one was injured or killed. Did your child get bullied at school today? This might be an excellent opportunity for him to learn how to deal with bullies. Reframing or restructuring your thinking is incredibly useful for dealing with what might otherwise consume your ability to be happy in a whirlwind of chronic worry.

EXERCISE: Use Cognitive Reframing

Take out your journal or write on a separate piece of paper. Try to reframe each of the following interpretations of reality in a more positive light.

1. "This traffic is hardly moving. At this rate, I'll get to work an hour or two from now. I might lose my job. I think I'm going to lose my mind if I have to sit here any longer."

2. "Tomorrow I have an exam. I'm so nervous. What if I fail?"

3. "It's now 8:00 p.m. and he still isn't home. He was supposed to be home at 5:00 p.m. What if he got into an accident and is dead or lying unconscious somewhere?"

4. "I have a doctor's appointment tomorrow to check to see if the cancer came back. It would be horrible if it came back and I needed more chemo. I don't know if I could take it again."

5. "I really had a good time tonight. But I don't know if he was that into me. What if he never asks me out again?"

Now write about something that you are or have been worried about. Write down what you are worried about and why you are worried about it. In other words, articulate your worry chain. Now construct a view of your worry that reframes your thinking in a more positive light.

Whenever you catch yourself beginning to worry, you can use cognitive reframing as an antidote.

Behavioral Antidotes

Behavioral antidotes are actions that correct irrational behavior. For example, if you are inclined to sit around and worry or refuse to go out of the house until you find a perfect solution to your problem (which is what dutiful worriers tend to do), a behavioral antidote would be to force yourself out of the house to do something else.

Thus, instead of sitting there needlessly ruminating, you can pick yourself up and go shopping or do something else you would like to do. Of course, this won't be easy, because you will have built up, over the years, resistance to stopping your worrying, and as you know, you'll tend to feel guilty if you try not to worry. In fact, you might feel guilty even about entertaining the thought of doing something other than worrying. Nevertheless, by pushing yourself to get involved in something else, you can distract yourself from your worrying and begin to cultivate more constructive habits.

The plain truth is that if you have less time to ruminate, you will do less of it. So getting busy can be a constructive antidote to the thinking that drives dutiful worrying. For example, if you are a stay-at-home mom and the high point in the day is when your kids come home from school, then you could bring more activities into your life that you enjoy and look forward to. One client who went back to work after eight years discovered that at work she tended to worry less about her children. Some of the family tension that was centered on worrying about the children began to diminish.

Changing your behavior can be an important part of overcoming your habit of worrying. In fact, when you act as if nothing were wrong, it can actually help you feel better. Have you ever felt down but had somewhere to go and couldn't get out of it? So you decided to go anyway and put on an act to hide how you really felt? Did you eventually start to feel better? Acting as if there were nothing wrong can provide at least some temporary relief from the stress of negative emotions.

Having a plan of action will also help. If you consciously give yourself a behavioral assignment, including specifying details such as time and place for implementation, you will be more likely to act on your decision to change your behavior. It is therefore important to include such a plan in constructing behavioral antidotes.

Often, there is an interval of time between coming to a rational decision and implementing it. This can be a challenging period when you will be ready to rehash your decision and to engage in worrying. Unless you are vigilant in stopping yourself from doing this, you may well end up abandoning your decision. So, in this interim period between making your rational decision and implementing it, you may want to construct a behavioral assignment to go out and do something that you enjoy doing. This will keep your mind off of your problem.

EXERCISE: Do a Behavioral Assignment

The next time you are worried about something (or right now if you are worried about something), give yourself a behavioral assignment to pretend that you are not worried about anything. Even if the prospect of not worrying leads you to feel guilty, do it anyway. Keep it up for at least three hours.

After you have completed your behavioral assignment, think about your experience and record your thoughts in your journal. What were you telling yourself while you were putting on your act? Were you committing any reasoning fallacies? Did you feel guilty? If so, did you feel more or less guilty as time elapsed? How did you feel immediately after completing this assignment? Did you feel better or worse than before you undertook this assignment?

Both cognitive and behavioral antidotes are central to the four-step program, and in later chapters you will have many opportunities to apply them.

A Cognitive Behavioral Approach

Perhaps one of the most important insights of contemporary psychology has been the realization that cognitive and behavioral interventions can work together synergistically to provide lasting relief from anxiety, depression, and other behavioral and emotional problems. This book's four-step program for overcoming dutiful worrying is based on this insight and systematically incorporates both cognitive and behavioral interventions. The following table sums up how this cognitive behavioral approach is implemented within the four-step program for overcoming dutiful worrying:

COGNITIVE BEHAVIORAL INTERVENTIONS WITHIN THE FOUR-STEP PROGRAM

Steps	How to Implement Each Step
Identify your faulty reasoning.	Find your worry chain by asking: "What am I worried about?" and "Why am I worried about this?" Use template to formulating your dutiful-worrying reasoning.
Refute your fallacies.	Use checklists to refute your fallacies (see chapter 4).
Take a rational approach.	Reframe your thinking: Construct a cognitive antidote for each reasoning fallacy. Make a rational decision. Construct behavioral antidotes: Make a behavioral plan to act upon your decision. Give yourself at least one behavioral assignment to do something you enjoy doing instead of worrying.
Use your willpower to stop worrying.	Exercise your willpower muscle to remind yourself of the refutations of your fallacies; enforce your cognitive antidotes; do your behavioral assignments; and implement your behavioral plan.

Steps 1 and 2 in this table are cognitive interventions, while step 3 has both cognitive and behavioral components. To take a rational approach, you first reframe your thinking by constructing a cognitive antidote for each of your refuted fallacies. Second, you make a rational decision to apply these cognitive antidotes. Employing these antidotes will help you to attain the moral virtues corresponding to each of the fallacies. Finally, you construct behavioral antidotes, including a behavioral plan to implement your rational decision and at least one enjoyable assignment. These behavioral antidotes will help you go on with your life instead of continuing to ruminate over your problem and rehash your decision. They can also help you to follow through with your decision.

Here's an example of how to take step 3. Suppose you realize that you are unrealistically demanding certainty. As a cognitive antidote to this behavior, you can tell yourself to accept an answer to your problem that is reasonable, even though it's no guarantee. This is an antidote for losing-control anxiety. Adhering to this antidote can help to build courage, for it requires you to take reasonable risks, which helps you to reach the golden mean in responding to danger.

In the light of this change in your thinking, you can make a rational decision, or come up with a reasonable solution to your problem. For example, you might decide to take a job offer even though it involves relocating and there is no guarantee that the job will work out. Then you would construct a behavioral plan to implement this decision You might give yourself the assignment to call your prospective employer at 9 o'clock the next morning to accept the job offer. Then you might give yourself one or more other enjoyable behavioral assignments to keep you from ruminating about the decision you've already made. For example, you might go shopping.

Following step 4, you might remind yourself about the refutations of your fallacies and why you should therefore refrain from committing these fallacies. For example, having made the decision to accept the job offer, you could remind yourself that it is unrealistic to demand certainty about this being the right choice, and then you could push yourself to fulfill both your cognitive and behavioral assignments. Thus you could enforce your cognitive antidote, telling yourself to have the courage to accept reasonable risks in order to move forward in life. You could also enforce your behavioral antidotes, such as pushing yourself to go shopping this evening and to make the phone call at 9:00 a.m. tomorrow to accept the job offer, as planned. In fact, it is such behavioral changes in conjunction with such cognitive changes that are most likely to help you stop worrying.

The next chapter presents some useful cognitive antidotes to losing-control anxiety that will enable you to reframe this self-disturbing thinking and cultivate, instead, a habit of courageously confronting your life issues.

CHAPTER 6

Cultivating Courage

When you dutifully worry, you are afraid that something catastrophic might happen unless you figure out a way to stop it. You experience losing-control anxiety, an excessive fear based on exaggeration of the risks, the seriousness of the stakes, and a misunderstanding about what you can and can't control.

On the other hand, exercising courage requires avoiding excessive fear and finding the golden mean between being too fearful or too foolhardy. Notice that this definition of courage does not require that you be fearless in all situations. This would be unreasonable. For example, if you were in the path of a Mack truck, then fear would be an appropriate response. On the other hand, if you are afraid to cross the street because you think that you might be run over by a car even when there is none in sight, then your fear is excessive and irrational. This is because you are exaggerating the probabilities of being run over when crossing the street.

Courageous people do sometimes worry, but not usually in excess. For example, worrying about what would happen to your children if you were not there to care for them may prompt you to execute a will and name your children as beneficiaries of your estate. However, if your worrying still continues even after you have taken reasonable action, then it is excessive and irrational.

Dutiful worrying always involves excessive and irrational fear. So exercising courage is never consistent with dutiful worrying. But, you may ask, don't courageous people have the duty to worry about important things like providing for their children?

The answer is no. Granted, you have a duty to provide for your children, but this does not mean that you have another duty to worry about providing for your children. While the former calls for taking constructive action (such as feeding, clothing, and educating them, and taking proper care of their health), the latter calls for you to upset yourself about providing for your children. You don't have to make yourself worry in order to provide for your children or to be a worthy parent (or person). In fact, chronic worrying will make it harder for you to act responsibly, because worrying will stress you out and make it harder for you to think rationally. As a dutiful worrier, it will take courage for you not to worry.

Applying Antidotes to Losing-Control Anxiety

You can overcome your dutiful-worrying fallacies and become morally virtuous by applying rational antidotes, prescriptive rules or guidelines that tell you how to avoid going to extremes (see chapter 5). Some antidotes prescribe behavior (behavioral antidotes), while others tell you how to change your thinking (cognitive antidotes). In the case of losing-control anxiety, cognitive antidotes tell you how to avoid being too afraid or not sufficiently afraid and accordingly help you to become courageous in confronting the things that you needlessly worry about.

This chapter will introduce you to the following potentially useful cognitive antidotes to losing-control anxiety:

+ Reframe in life-affirming terms the things you fear the most, such as death.

+ Look upon your life challenges as opportunities to learn, grow, and become stronger.

+ Think of something much worse than your present situation, and bear in mind that your situation is not as bad as this.

+ Assess risks and probabilities on the basis of evidence, not on how much you fear something.

+ Live by probability, not by certainty.

+ Replace Murphy's Law with the principle of evidence.

+ Distinguish between what is and what is not in your power to control, and accept your limitations.

+ Avoid using catastrophic language such as "terrible," "horrible," "awful," and "the worst," and instead use words such as "tough break," "unfortunate," and "bad."

As you work on attaining courage, you may find some of these antidotes more relevant than others, so you can simply use the antidotes that most suit you.

Reframe in Life-Affirming Terms What You Fear the Most

Death is final and permanent, and there is nothing you can do about it when someone dies. So the thought of yourself or a loved one dying can be a daunting thought. However, many dutiful worriers fear death most of all and spend countless hours of their lives worrying needlessly about this ultimate fate and how to prevent it from happening. If there is even a remote chance of being fatally injured or of a loved one being fatally injured, then this may be fodder for dutiful worrying. One problem with such thinking, however, is that death is a fact of life, and it is therefore not possible to eliminate it completely without ceasing to live in the world.

But just how fearful of death should we be? Many philosophers have pointed out that the price of life is the possibility of death. If a ship owner wanted to play it safe, said Saint Thomas Aquinas, he would always keep his ship in port. Sailing the sea of life has risks, but it is what turns human existence into a living adventure. If you are not prepared to tolerate the prospect of death, then you simply can't live a fulfilled life.

The sage Epicurus said that "death, the most dreaded of evils, should not concern us, for while we exist death is not present, and when death is present, we no longer exist. It is therefore nothing either to the living or to the dead since it is not present to the living, and the dead no longer are" (2003, 251). Such a reframing of death can help to take the edge off its ferocity. Still, what may be present to the living when a loved one dies is the unalterable reality that a loved one has died.

It is sometimes said that you are not an adult until you experience the death of a loved one. Indeed, working through such a loss can be one of the more challenging things we have to confront in living and growing older. But you haven't fully worked through the death if you haven't stopped damning yourself, damning the universe, or telling yourself how you can't stand to live with such an awful fact. It is through the expression of such judgments—and later, when you are ready, the inspection of them—that you can come to see their irrationality: it is not your fault; the world still has good things in it to look forward to; you can stand to live; and as unfortunate as the death may have been, it is still not the end of world. This is a useful and enlightened perspective about life to learn from death. Having so worked through a death does indeed provide an initiation into the world of rational adults.

Experiencing the death of a loved one can also point to the importance of living life to its fullest. This includes not worrying your life away. Far from having a duty to worry about death, it arguably makes more sense to suppose that you have a duty to make the best of your life while you can. As Epicurus admonished, the prudent person doesn't live in fear of dying. Instead, just as such a person doesn't choose the most food but rather the food that is the most pleasant, "so he does not seek the enjoyment of the longest life but of the happiest" (2003, 251). In other words, it is the quality of life that counts the most, not how long that life lasts.

In my practice as a clinical medical ethicist, I help medical staff, patients, and their families to reach decisions when hard ethical choices must be made, oftentimes ones that concern death and dying. In my work, I have seen patients who have lost basic qualities that make life worth living—the ability to think, to communicate, to laugh, and even to cry. Yet life in such a vegetative state can persist for weeks, months, and years. Reflecting for a moment about cases of this nature can serve to remind you not to take for granted the quality of your life. Spending much of your life preoccupied with the risks of yourself or someone you love dying is self-defeating because it neglects the very qualities that make life worth living in the first place.

This does not mean that you should roll the dice without regard for life and limb. But you must not be too afraid to live. Life is enhanced through activities, not through living in a bubble.

The prospect of your own demise can be a formidable obstacle to your happiness if you let it. One client, who was a young woman, worried so much about dying that she was afraid to live. She even told herself that there is no point to life if you are going to die anyway. As a result she was depressed. What she needed to do was to reframe her view of death.

Again, death can be more constructively viewed as a wakeup call to live life to its fullest while you can. As the French existential thinker Jean-Paul Sartre explained, the fact of your mortality is part of the human condition into which you are born. How you deal with this fact is up to you. However, a person who is too afraid to live in the face of death succeeds only in defining herself as "a disappointed dream, as miscarried hopes, as vain expectations" (2000, 447). You are, said Sartre, the sum total of your actions. Without acting, you shortchange yourself and make your life less rather than more.

Indeed, death can be viewed as the starting point of life. Because you are going to die, you should choose to live. The following exercise will help you stop worrying about death, yours and that of those whom you love, and start to live and let live.

EXERCISE: Reframe Your View of Death

Take a pen or pencil and record your answers to the following questions: Does a significant amount of your worrying (directly or indirectly) center around preventing or mitigating the possibility of death, either your own or that of others? What is your philosophy of death? How do you see it in relation to life? Do you dread death? How does the prospect of your own mortality affect the way you live? How does it affect the way you relate to loved ones?

Now construct a few sentences describing how the fact of death may actually affirm the value of life and why it doesn't demand that you live in fear of dying. This will provide you with a cognitive antidote to losing-control anxiety that you can use in cultivating courage. Be prepared to use it to reframe your thinking if and when you find yourself worrying excessively about death or dying.

Look Upon Life's Challenges As Opportunities for Growth

In affirming life, you can also affirm the challenges that life brings. Rather than seeing these challenges as obstacles, you can see them as opportunities to prosper. To an extent, danger and risk are a part of life. Sanitizing life by stripping away the elements of risk and danger would make for a boring existence. This does not mean you ought to take foolish risks, however. If you are prone to go to extremes, then be careful that you don't simply shift from one extreme to the other—from being too afraid to being not afraid enough. That won't make you courageous either.

On the other hand, you can learn and grow from life's challenges even if you have a negative experience. As the British philosopher David Hume (2003) remarked, all people and even other animals learn about things in the world by observation. Without learning from the past, we would have no basis for making judgments about the future.

Even misfortunes can open up new opportunities to grow. In the fall of 2004, my hometown of Port Saint Lucie, Florida, was struck by two consecutive hurricanes within three weeks of one another. Hurricane Francis caused widespread devastation, and Hurricane Jean put the finishing touches on it. In this process, my house was destroyed and we lost about half of our personal property.

Amid the devastation, life as we knew it came to a halt. There was no electricity, no running water (since we depended on electric pumps), and no fresh meat or produce. Eventually some supermarkets opened and supplied canned goods on a limited basis. Construction workers were at a premium, and it was difficult to start the arduous effort of rebuilding. There was widespread looting of abandoned homes, and people who had generators had to guard them.

As a result of my experience, however, I now know better the value of things once taken for granted. I never thought much about the value of a kitchen sink or a place to bathe or a dwelling that wasn't infested with hundreds of thousands of mold spores. I didn't appreciate as I do now a visit to my local supermarket. I never appreciated the value of a (nonleaky) roof over my head as much as I do now. The loss of personal possessions, from old photos to books damaged by mold, gave me a new perspective on the transient nature of things of value. Yet in the immediate aftermath of the hurricanes, it never occurred to me that I was learning to be a stronger, more enlightened person.

The truth is that what may seem like a formidable obstacle to our happiness or to the happiness of others whom we love can turn out to have significant positive value, even though this value may not be immediately evident. Looking back at what happened tends to change the level of ferocity. With time, we gain perspective and wisdom. Our life encounters with rejection, failure, betrayal, death, destruction, and material loss tend to shape the people whom we later become.

"Profound suffering," said Friedrich Nietzsche, "makes noble" and "separates" the sufferer from the uninitiated (1954, 596). This is not a justification for deliberately staging tragic events or putting yourself in the path of a natural disaster. But it does point out that intense fear can obscure the nature of reality, which is not all bad. Having courage means seeing risk and danger in this broader context of life, with its good as well as bad possibilities, and being willing to live, learn, and grow from your experiences.

EXERCISE: Learn from the Past

Make a list of several things that you have learned from your past mistakes. In your estimation, looking back, were any or all of these mistakes worth having made?

What is one of the worst things you have experienced in your life? Make a list of any negative events from which you have learned something important.

The next time you experience losing-control anxiety, you can think about how you have previously learned from your past challenges and try reframing your present situation as an opportunity to learn and grow.

Think of Something Much Worse Than the Present

When I reflect on the devastating earthquake that struck Haiti or the onslaught of Hurricane Katrina in New Orleans, I see that the losses I suffered were not nearly the magnitude of those suffered by the victims of these disasters. The upshot is that misfortune is boundless. Things can always get worse.

In the midst of fearing what you perceive to be impending doom, it can be helpful to reframe your situation by focusing on a worse possibility. You may say to yourself: *What's going to happen if I lose my job? What am I going to do if they raise my automobile insurance rates as a result of that accident? How am I going to get through to that troubled teenager of mine? What am I going to do if we get divorced?*

Understandably, you care about being gainfully employed, being able to afford automobile insurance, the well-being of your teenager, and your marriage. But it is easy to get caught up in worrying about such things, put them under a magnifying glass, and build them up in your mind to catastrophic proportions.

In the midst of such catastrophizing, it may seem as if you were facing the crisis of your life, and you may not feel like putting the situation into a broader perspective. This is because it is easier to go with the flow of your old thinking than to go against it by reframing your thinking. However, putting things in perspective is exactly what you should do: *Well, even if I lost my job, it wouldn't be as bad as being blacklisted and never being able to work again. Even if my auto insurance goes up, it would have been a lot worse if someone had been fatally injured in that accident. Yes, it's hard getting through to that teenager of mine, but there are worse situations. What if my child had a life-threatening disease like cancer? Okay, so it's not so great that our marriage isn't working out, but there are, after all, a lot worse things. I could have married a homicidal maniac who was trying to kill me instead of divorce me.*

Such lines of self-talk can help you see that the undesirable things that preoccupy you have only a relative negative worth and not an absolute one, that misfortune admits of degrees, and that what you fear is by no means the worst possible thing that could happen.

EXERCISE: Learn to Appreciate That Things Could Be Much Worse

Try doing the following:

1. Think of something that you are (or have) worried about, which you regard (or have regarded) as awful or extremely bad.

2. Think of something that would be (or would have been) much worse.

3. Imagine that this much worse thing is really happening at this moment. That is, try to make yourself feel the way you would feel if it were true.

4. Compare what you were worried about with the much worse thing that you just imagined was real.

5. How do you feel now? Does what you were (or have been) worried about seem quite as bad as it did before?

The next time you experience losing-control anxiety, you can repeat this exercise to get some perspective on what you are worrying about.

Assess Risks and Probabilities on the Basis of Evidence

There are two reasonable questions to ask when determining how bad something may be:

1. How harmful would the consequences be?

2. How likely are these consequences to occur?

A harm that is remotely possible is not as bad as one that is imminent. Dutiful worriers tend to either overrate the seriousness of the harm or magnify the risks of its happening, or both. So you might catastrophize about something that is possible but very unlikely. One client, Nancy, worried about the possible side effects of giving her children antibiotics prescribed by her family physician when they were ill. On the package insert of one such drug, amoxicillin (a form of penicillin), she read,

> *Warnings: serious and occasionally fatal hypersensitivity*
> *(anaphylactic) reactions have been reported in patients on penicillin*
> *therapy. Although anaphylaxis is more frequent following parenteral*
> *[injected] therapy, it has occurred in patients on oral penicillin.*
> *These reactions are more likely to occur in individuals with a*
> *history of penicillin hypersensitivity and/or a history of sensitivity to*
> *multiple allergens.*

Despite the fact that Nancy's children had no history of penicillin hypersensitivity or relevant food or drug allergies, every time one of her children went on the medication she feared that the child was going to suffer anaphylactic shock and die.

Was it possible that the feared consequence could really happen? Yes, it was possible. Was it probable? No. The fatality rate has been estimated to be one case in every 50,000 to 100,000 administered courses of penicillin (Rieder 1994). Indeed, the fact that millions of dosages are safely administered, coupled with the fact that her children were receiving the drug orally and had no known predisposing factors, made Nancy's fear excessive. While the possibility existed, it was highly unlikely.

Nor could Nancy's fear count as evidence. The truth is not directly proportional to the extent of your fear. In fact, intense fear can obscure the search for truth. Unfortunately, many dutiful worriers think that somehow what they fear the most is the most likely to happen. Thus, Nancy loved her children dearly, so much that her fear of losing a child was, for her, good enough reason to worry. Yet she had no medical basis to support her fear, and the fear itself couldn't substitute for such evidence.

EXERCISE: Base Your Probability Claims on Evidence

Make a list of things that at some point in your life you thought were highly likely to happen even if they never happened. The more things you can add to your list, the better, but try to include at least five things. Now ask yourself if you had convincing evidence to back up your claim that each of the things on your list would probably happen. Examine each item on the list. If you can answer "yes, I had evidence," then write down the evidence that you had at the time. This evidence would have to be facts that you verified—for example, you consulted a reliable source, such as a study conducted by credible scientists.

Fearing that something might happen is inadequate evidence. The next time you predict that something will happen, make sure that your prediction is based on evidence and not fear.

Live by Probability, Not by Certainty

Even the remote possibility of such a horrific thing happening as the death of a child was, for Nancy, something to worry about. She did not want to hear that the dreaded consequence was "unlikely." She demanded certainty in order to refrain from worrying. However, in this imperfect world, the demand for certainty is plainly unrealistic.

What Nancy needed to do, therefore, was to give up her demand for certainty and to live by probability: *Yes, there is a remote possibility that the medicine could cause anaphylaxis, but there is an even greater risk that the untreated infection could have untoward consequences, so I'll go with the medicine.* This is what it means to live by probability. It is about weighing risks and benefits with the understanding that whatever decision you make carries some degree of risk. If you think like this, you will at least avoid the anxiety of demanding certainty in a world that does not provide it.

EXERCISE: Proportion Your Beliefs to the Degree of Evidence

Do the following:

1. Think of something you've worried a lot about that you thought was likely to happen. Did the fact that you were afraid of this thing happening influence your thinking that it was likely to happen?

2. Make a list of the three things you worry about the most.

3. For each of the three items on your list, write down the evidence you have for thinking it might happen.

4. In your estimation, does the evidence in each case support a conclusion that it is likely to happen?

5. For each of your three worries, are you disturbed by the thought of something happening even if the possibility of what you fear is remote? That is, are you demanding certainty before you will stop worrying?

The next time you experience losing-control anxiety, you can ask yourself if you are demanding certainty before you stop worrying. If so, you can remind yourself to proportion your beliefs to the degree of evidence.

Replace Murphy's Law with the Principle of Evidence

Many dutiful worriers also subscribe to Murphy's Law, which says that anything that can go wrong will go wrong. However, this is to fly in the face of reason, because many things that can go wrong simply don't. For example, the last time you drove your car, it was possible for the brakes to have failed, but they didn't. Indeed, consider how many things you rely on in the course of a day to function efficiently and which function as expected. Murphy's Law is therefore an unduly pessimistic perspective that is not based on evidence. Wipe Murphy's Law from your standards of belief and replace it with the principle of basing your beliefs on the evidence.

EXERCISE: Refute Murphy's Law

Do you subscribe to Murphy's Law? Can you think of something that you have worried would go wrong but actually never did? If so, you have refuted Murphy's Law as a basis for worrying.

The next time you start to worry that something will probably go wrong, remember to refute Murphy's law.

Do Not Try to Control What Is Not in Your Power to Control

Along with accepting the limits of certainty, you should also accept the limits of your control over things. As the Stoic Epictetus warned, there are some things that you can control and some things you can't. Among the things that are under your control are reframing or interpreting reality, choosing, desiring, disliking, and other thinking activities. Among the things not under your control are whether other people will approve of you, whether you will lose your money (say in a business venture) or your job, and other things that are not of your own doing.

According to Epictetus (2009), if you confuse these two sets of things, and think you can control what you can't control, you will live in a state of anxiety, whereas if you stick to trying to control only what's really in your power to control, you will avoid this needless stress. Epictetus illustrates how such needless stress can arise with the case of a musician who feels no anxiety when he is singing only for himself but feels anxious in front of an audience, even if he is performing well. The musician feels anxious partly because he wants to perform well and partly because he wants the audience's applause, even though the audience's approval or disapproval of his performance is something he cannot control.

Similarly, you can worry dutifully about things not in your control and thereby have an unrealistic fear of losing control. Your fear is unrealistic because the object of your fear, that of losing control, does not even exist. Again, you cannot lose control over something that is not under your control in the first place. So your dutiful worrying is needless. Certainty is not something you can have; it is not something you can control, so it is self-defeating to try.

As the example of the musician also suggests, when you worry about getting the approval of others, you set yourself up for anxiety, for the approval of others is not something you can control. Of course, you can control your performance, but in the end, whether or not the members of the audience respond favorably is a function of factors that are beyond your control, including their state of mind, their individual tastes, and their enculturation. This is why it doesn't pay to worry about whether others will approve of you.

In fact, many dutiful worriers worry about getting the approval of others. You might catastrophize and tell yourself that you would be a bad or worthless person if you failed to get it. As a result, you can set yourself up to feel guilty when you are not worrying about what others might think of you and then tell yourself that you have to worry. This thinking is self-defeating and anxiety producing.

EXERCISE: Distinguish Between What You Can and Can't Control

Review your list of three things that you worry about most (from the Degree of Evidence exercise), and then answer the following:

1. Using the distinction that Epictetus makes between things you can and can't control, into which category do each of the objects of your three worries fall?

2. Which aspects of each of your three worries are in your power to control and which aspects are not? For example, as in the

case of the musician, you may be able to control how well you perform but not be able to control the audience's response.

3. What are the most worrisome aspects of your three worries, the things you can control or the things you can't?

The next time you start to worry, remember that it's better to plan for what you can control and not worry about what you can't.

Avoid Using Catastrophic Language

When people catastrophize, they typically use strong negative emotive language, saying such words as "awful," "horrible," "terrible," and "the worst" to describe what might occur. These words do not merely describe or report events, but rather they prescribe or direct you to feel intense anxiety about the objects to which they are applied.

The expression "This is horrible" is far more intense than "This is unfortunate." Saying that a situation is "challenging" or "difficult" or even "a bad thing" makes it sound much more manageable than saying that it is "the worst thing that could have happened."

The choice of language is yours to make. Language has power, but you have power over language. You can pick and choose your own words. If you are selective, you can avoid making yourself needlessly afraid. By eliminating catastrophic language from your vocabulary, you can help yourself to avoid considerable anxiety.

EXERCISE: Replace Your Catastrophic Language

Do the following:

1. Make a list of the language that you tend to use when you catastrophize about bad things happening.

2. Make a new list of less emotively charged language that you can use to replace your catastrophic language.

3. Think about one of your biggest worries in the catastrophic terms you are accustomed to using, and allow yourself to feel the anxiety you would ordinarily feel while ruminating about this worry. Then change your language and think about your worry in the new language you have just generated.

4. Is there any difference in how you feel when you change your language? If there is, make a note of it in your journal.

Whenever you find yourself starting to catastrophize, you can replace your catastrophic language with terms from your new language.

Applying the Antidotes to Losing-Control Anxiety

You have now learned some useful cognitive antidotes to help you overcome the losing-control anxiety that propels dutiful worrying. At this point, you should be able to begin practicing going through each of the four steps to overcome your worrying, so you can see how these antidotes work in context. The more antidotes you get under your belt, the more virtues you will be able to work on; chapters 7 and 8 will concentrate on the virtues of self-respect and serenity. But for now you should be in a position to work on building courage.

The following is a courage-building exercise that will take you through some important aspects of the four steps for overcoming dutiful worrying. You should do this exercise whenever you start to worry about something that seems major and you feel anxious about it.

EXERCISE: Build Courage

Take each of the following steps to overcome your losing-control anxiety and build courage.

Step 1: Identify your faulty reasoning. First, find your worry chain. Remember to ask yourself what you are worried about. And then keep asking yourself why you are worried about it until you have constructed your full worry chain. Remember that the chain ends with something that you are worried about for its own sake.

After you have articulated your worry chain, identify your dutiful-worrying reasoning, using the following template to express your two premises and conclusion:

1. "If I don't keep worrying about [insert first link here], I won't be able to control things and [insert last link here] might happen." (losing-control anxiety)

2. Then I'd be a bad person for having let [insert last link here] happen." (self-damnation)

3. "So, I have to keep worrying about [insert first link here] until I'm certain I've found the best solution to it." (dutiful perfectionism)

As indicated above, take each of the blank spaces in the template to refer to the first and last links in the worry chain you just constructed and play out the resulting reasoning in your mind. That is, say it quietly to yourself.

Step 2: Refute the fallacies in your thinking. Use the following checklist to note any of these fallacies in the first premise of your reasoning:

☐ You are magnifying risks.

☐ You are exaggerating just how bad your situation really is relative to much worse things.

☐ You are demanding that you control something that is not in your power to control.

Recall that by checking off any item on this list, you have satisfactorily refuted your losing-control anxiety, because you have shown yourself exactly what is wrong with it.

Step 3. Take a rational approach. To build courage, find some cognitive antidotes to your losing-control anxiety. Choose two or more cognitive antidotes from among those you've learned in this chapter and apply your chosen antidotes to your worry. For example, if you have chosen to avoid controlling things that are not in your control, then distinguish between things that are and are not in your control. Ask yourself if what you are trying to control is really in your control, and if it's not, give yourself permission to give up trying to control it. Or if you have chosen to find something that is much worse than what you are worrying about, think of something worse and then keep in mind that your situation is not nearly as bad as this other, much worse situation. After you do these cognitive exercises, give yourself a behavioral assignment to do something that you enjoy doing. For example, you might have lunch with a friend or go shopping and buy that dress you've been coveting. The choice is yours, as long as you choose something you usually enjoy doing.

Step 4. Use your willpower to stop worrying. Make yourself do your behavioral assignment now (or as soon as you can) even if you don't feel like doing it. If you start to feel guilty, repeat step 2 and apply and follow your selected antidotes. Focus your attention on doing your behavioral assignment and enjoy yourself!

Now congratulate yourself. You've taken an important step to overcome your losing-control anxiety, and you deserve to feel good about it.

Completing the previous exercise is a milestone in working on overcoming your dutiful worrying, and it's important to have completed it before going on to subsequent chapters. Remember not to demand perfection. With continued practice, you will keep improving upon your skills and honing your virtues.

In the following chapters, you will continue in the four-step program for overcoming your dutiful worrying by working on building other moral virtues. In the next chapter, you will learn some antidotes to self-damnation, which can help you to develop unconditional self-respect.

CHAPTER 7

Respecting Yourself

When people dutifully worry, they not only fear that something catastrophic may happen unless they figure out how to stop it, but they also tell themselves that it would be their fault if this catastrophe occurred and so they must keep worrying. So far, you have learned how to identify and refute the fallacies in your dutiful-worrying reasoning, namely losing-control anxiety, self-damnation, and dutiful perfectionism. You have also begun to reframe your thinking by constructing cognitive antidotes to each of these reasoning fallacies. This chapter will show you in more depth how to construct cognitive antidotes to self-damnation.

Cognitive Antidotes to Self-Damnation

As you have seen, cognitive reframing can help you to cultivate moral virtues. In chapter 6 you were introduced to some cognitive antidotes specific to losing-control anxiety, which helped you to attain the moral virtue of courage. This chapter will introduce you to the following cognitive antidotes to self-damnation, which will help you to attain the virtue of unconditional self-respect:

- ◆ Think of your self-worth as unconditional, not as something that changes with successes, failures, or approval and disapproval of others.

- ◆ Whenever you begin to question your self-worth, remind yourself to keep the distinction between persons and objects straight.

- ◆ Don't call yourself or others degrading names.

- ◆ Stop second-guessing your ability to handle a situation or task at hand by demanding absolute assurance that you won't make a mistake.

- ◆ Love yourself as your own best friend.

The rest of this chapter will explain how these antidotes work. As you focus on attaining unconditional self-respect, you will want to apply the antidotes that most suit you.

Think of Your Self-Worth As Unconditional

Your self-worth does not change with successes, failures, or the approval or disapproval of others but is unconditional. This is important for dutiful worriers to remember, since dutiful worriers have a tendency to damn themselves.

Self-damnation is by its nature conditional. That is, it portrays your self-worth as dependent on certain states or conditions. To see this, here's a look at some major classes of self-damnation.

Achievement Damnation

One common class of self-damnation is that of *achievement damnation*. This kind of damnation involves berating yourself as unworthy (that is, as totally or almost totally devoid of worth) because you have, in your estimation, failed to perform adequately in some way or other. For example, some people perceive themselves as unworthy because their marriages did not work out or because they never did get married; others see themselves as unworthy because they have lost their jobs; others because they performed poorly (or at least not up to their own standards) at work or school; others because, as athletes, their game was off or they lost a competition or otherwise did not meet their athletic goals.

Many who engage in achievement damnation set perfectionistic goals that are impossible to meet. Then they condemn themselves for having failed. This is also a characteristic of dutiful worriers insofar as they unrealistically demand control over what is beyond their control. For example, a mom with whom I once worked sought to ensure that her children never got sick. So she worried constantly when her children came in contact with sick children, required them to carry disinfectant, and spent much of her time reading about outbreaks of infectious diseases, side effects of vaccinations, food recalls, and a host of other potential threats to her children's health. "How could I, in good conscience, not protect my kids from these things!" she exclaimed. But as you might expect, her children still caught colds, got respiratory infections, suffered allergy attacks, sprained their ankles, and so on. Unfortunately, each time a child got sick, she found some reason to blame herself for it and to question her self-worth.

EXERCISE: Identify the Bases of Your Achievement Damnation

Fill in the blank in the following statement to accurately reflect the basis on which you rate your self-worth:

If I don't perform well at or achieve _____,
then my rating of my self-worth is diminished.

See if you can come up with a list of things that you could place in the blank space. The list might include your productivity at work or school, parenting skills, athletic goals, or anything else that you think would make the statement true. This list represents the basis on which you are inclined to devaluate or damn yourself when you don't perform well or achieve your goals.

___

Approval Damnation

A further class of self-damnation is *approval damnation*, which involves thinking yourself unworthy because you failed to get the approval of another person (or persons). For example, some people seek the approval of a parent as a condition of their self-worth; others, approval of peers; others, their employer; and others, their friends. Typically, people who engage in approval damnation do not require the approval of everyone as a condition of their self-worth. They rather require the approval of a select individual or class of individuals. So, you may not care whether your teacher approves of you or your work, but you might see yourself as unworthy if your friends do not approve of you.

In fact, achievement damnation is not infrequently based on approval damnation. That is, many people want to accomplish their goals so that they can receive the approval or acceptance of certain others. Dutiful worriers may sometimes be most afraid of losing the approval or acceptance of certain people who are special to them. This is important to note, because in filling out your worry chains, you may be leaving out what you are most afraid of in the end, namely falling into the disfavor of others.

EXERCISE: Identify the Bases of Your Approval Damnation

Fill in the blank in the following statement, naming anyone you can think of whose approval you seek as a condition of your rating of your self-worth.

If I don't get or keep the approval of _____,
then my rating of my self-worth is diminished.

If you do, in fact, engage in approval damnation, then you should be able to generate such a list of people without whose approval you are inclined to devalue or damn yourself.

Moral Damnation

A related class of self-damnation is *moral damnation*. In this case, people think themselves unworthy because they perceive themselves as having committed a moral transgression (violated a moral principle). People often express this kind of self-damnation by calling themselves bad. For example, you tell yourself that you are a bad person because you didn't visit your mother enough when she was ill; or because you got arrested; or because you lied; or because you cheated on your partner.

While dutiful worriers may engage in all three kinds of self-damnation described above, the dominant form is moral. That is, as a dutiful worrier, you may even see failure to achieve your goals or to receive the approval of others as moral failures. For example, many dutiful worriers are inclined to damn themselves when they think that they have lost the confidence of loved ones or friends. So your self-damning tendency may be based on your demand for approval from these special people, but you may also view your failure to satisfy this demand as itself a moral failure: *What kind of person would let his friends down?* Insofar as you think losing the confidence or approval of your friends is a moral failure, you will feel guilty if you try to avoid worrying about it.

EXERCISE: Identify Your Moral Damnation

Fill in the blank in the following statement with anything that you think is or would be morally wrong, anything that you have worried about, and anything else that you think diminishes or would diminish your self-worth.

My doing or failing to do _____
diminishes, or would, in my opinion, diminish my self-worth.

Write down not only things that you have actually done but also things that you might have thought of doing or were afraid you might do. For example, have you ever worried about doing something (or failing to do something) that would result in serious harm to a loved one? Anything on this list is a perceived moral offense on the basis of which you tend to devaluate or damn yourself.

Do any of the things on your list involve the loss of or failure to get approval from someone else? For example, perhaps you think that you have betrayed a friend and thus lost her approval. If so, do any of these people also appear on your list of people whose approval you depend on for your self-worth (see previous exercise)? If so, then attaining or keeping the approval of these people is probably a significant source of your dutiful worrying.

Unconditional Self-Respect

As you can see, when people damn themselves, they make their self-worth conditional upon something else—their achievements, the approval of others, or the moral propriety of their actions. This conditionality can create major life stress. That is, as long as you are achieving what you want, gaining the approval of certain others, or acting in morally appropriate ways, you can continue to rate yourself as a worthy person. On the other hand, as soon as you fail to live up to these demands, your sense of self-worth will plummet. Moreover, even when you are meeting these conditions for your self-worth, you are still likely to feel anxious about the prospect of losing your self-worth in the future: *What happens if I stop performing well at work? What happens if my friends decide they don't like me anymore? What happens if I screw up and do something wrong again? Then what good would I be anyway?*

In this way, people who engage in self-damnation do not permit themselves to be at ease, for, at any time, their self-worth and hence the merit of their very existence can be called into question. It is this conditionality of self-worth that sustains and intensifies the anxiety of dutiful worrying: *What if I fail to control things and awful things happen? Then it would be my fault and I would be a worthless person. So I just can't stop thinking about this and let myself relax.*

But you can take yourself off this anxiety-ridden roller coaster ride. You can do this by reframing your view of your own self-worth as unconditional. To do this, you need to give up the self-defeating idea that your self-worth comes and goes with the addition or subtraction of your achievements, others' approval, or whether you think you have acted morally.

This does not mean that you should never be critical of your own misconduct. There is an important practical difference between condemning the deed and condemning the doer. In condemning yourself, you have sealed your own fate. You have decided that you are unworthy of future happiness. On the other hand, condemning your action is quite consistent with your future happiness. Unfortunately, dutiful worrying thrives on condemning the doer: *What a bad person I'd be if I let that happen!*

So as an antidote to self-damnation, think of your self-worth as unconditional and therefore as something that can never be taken away from you. In this way, you can stop yourself from basing your self-worth on your achievements, the approval of others, and the moral appropriateness of your actions.

In the previous exercises in this chapter, you have hopefully gotten a clearer idea of the bases of your own self-damnation and where you need to remind yourself that your self-worth is unconditional. For example, if you berate yourself on the basis of whether or not you achieve the goals you have set for yourself, then you can tell yourself that your value does not depend on your achievements. If your self-abasement is based on your demand for approval, then you can tell yourself that your self-worth is independent of whether or not anyone approves of you. Likewise, if you engage in moral self-abasement, then you can tell yourself to keep the moral propriety of your actions separate from your worthiness. You can tell yourself that you are still a worthy person regardless of whether you have done bad things. You can always change your actions in the future because you are still a worthy person with the capacity for improvement.

Indeed, the inference from "I did some bad things" to "I am bad" is clearly unsound, for if doing bad things made you bad, then we'd all be bad, inasmuch as all of us have done bad things. So separate the doer from the deed. Your self-worth is always unconditional even if the merit of your deeds may be not.

EXERCISE: Reframe Your Self-Worth As Unconditional

Based on the lists you have generated in the previous three exercises, how would you characterize your tendencies to engage in self-damnation? Do you berate yourself based on your achievements; on the approval from certain others; on your moral appraisal?

Now take the following two steps:

1. Think of an example of your self-damnation. For example, if you tend to berate yourself if you don't get the approval of a certain person, think about a particular situation in which you berated yourself based on your being unable to get approval from that person (or persons).

2. Now reframe your thinking. That is, tell yourself that your self-worth does not depend on this basis. For example, tell yourself that you are a worthy person regardless of whether this person approves of you, because your self-worth is unconditional. Recall the difference between condemning the deed and condemning the doer. So even if you think you made a mistake or did something wrong, remind yourself that you are still a worthy person.

Repeat these two steps for any other examples of self-damnation that you can recall.

Whenever you find yourself caught up in self-damnation, you can use this exercise to reframe your self-worth as unconditional. This can help you to build and strengthen the habit and moral virtue of unconditional self-respect.

Remember That You Are a Person, Not an Object

Again, when people damn themselves, they treat their worth as though it were dependent on personal achievements, approval ratings, and morally appropriate conduct. But again, this is confusing the doer with the deed. Another way of looking at this is to say that when people damn themselves, they are treating themselves like an object, for objects are valuable insofar as they are useful. Thus, a pen is as valuable as its usefulness for writing. When the pen stops writing (say because its cartridge gets used up), the pen is thrown away. Its value is therefore totally dependent on its utility. Similarly, you might get rid of a dress if it were no longer considered stylish to wear.

In contrast, people are not pens or a dress to be thrown away or discarded when no longer of a particular use. This is because human beings have an unconditional worth or value. The eighteenth-century German philosopher Immanuel Kant (1964) pointed out that this value can be neither increased nor diminished by a person's usefulness or whether others accept or reject him. Instead, a human being's worth is unconditional; it is a constant, not a variable.

As Kant explained, objects are different from people because they are not capable of self-determination. That is, people can make reasoned decisions about what they want to do, where they want to go, and how they want to be treated. So their actions are autonomous, or determined from within by a process of reasoning. In contrast, the fate of objects is determined by outside sources. Thus, you determine what to do with the pen, where to place it, and how it will otherwise be used.

When you damn yourself, you are denying the value, worth, and dignity you have by virtue of being a person. So, instead of telling yourself that your self-worth depends on whether you achieve some goal, gain someone's approval, or act in a certain way, you should tell yourself that you are a worthy person regardless of any such conditions. You are worthy, not because you meet any particular external standards but because you are a full-fledged person, a rational self-determining being who, as such, has worth and dignity in your own right.

So when you are worrying about something potentially not going right and holding yourself responsible for that possibility, you should remind yourself that you are a person, not an object. Just as you would not want to treat other people as objects, you should not want to treat yourself as one.

You can tell yourself this instead: *I am worthy even if I mess up, even if I fall short of the demands I make on myself, and even if I do not attain the approval of others that I desire. I have unconditional self-worth and dignity because I am a person, a self-determining rational being—not some object to be used up and thrown out.*

To see just how important this distinction between a person and an object is, consider the case of some former clients, a group of displaced homemakers.

• The Displaced Homemakers

A group of middle-aged women, all of whom were recently divorced or widowed, had spent all or most of their adult lives tending to household chores, raising children, and catering to the wants of their husbands. They had been brought up to believe that the place of a woman was in the home, and they unquestion-ingly did what was expected of them.

However, after their husbands were no longer in their lives and their children were grown, all this changed. These women now felt as though they no longer had any purpose in life, for they had defined themselves in terms of their role as wife and mother, and now one role was gone and the other much diminished.

These women needed to reframe the way they perceived their self-worth. They needed to see that they were not objects whose worth was exhausted by their usefulness. The French existentialist thinker Jean-Paul Sartre made this point by saying that, for human beings, "existence precedes essence" (2000, 444). Objects, Sartre maintained, are designed with preset pur-poses. For example, a paper cutter is designed by the inventor to cut paper and that is what it is created for. The factory has a blueprint ("essence") for the product prior to its existence, and then it is produced according to this idea. In contrast, human beings are not created according to a preset idea of what they are intended to do. Instead, we have free will and can define our own purposes. Thus, it was always possible for the displaced home-makers to redefine themselves by changing their goals or aspirations. This was indeed what these women needed to do in order to be fulfilled.

So, in line with Sartre, I talked with them about their free will and their ability to set new goals for themselves, and I encouraged them to set and pursue new educational, career, and social goals. Clearly, these women had to work hard both cognitively and behaviorally to overcome the inertia of their prior socialization that kept them entrenched in the archaic idea that their only place was in the home. The last time I checked, most of these women were on their way toward building new and productive lives. However, this was possible only by surrendering the idea that they were like objects whose worth was bound up with a preset purpose.

Does the story of these homemakers sound familiar to you? Have you ever made your value contingent on your usefulness to others?

EXERCISE: Reframe Yourself As a Person

Think of as many ways as you can when you have objectified yourself by making your value dependent on your use or purpose. For example, do you make your worth contingent on how good a homemaker or mother you are? Or on how well you do your job? If you don't do something perfectly well, do you worry that you will be worthless? Have you ever felt worthless after losing a job or hearing that you were no longer needed for something? Now remind yourself that you are not an object whose worth depends on how useful you are. That is, you are not like an old shoe that can be discarded when it no longer serves a set purpose. Rather, you are a person, a rational self-determining being who deserves respect quite apart from any use you may serve.

Don't Call Yourself or Others Degrading Names

As discussed in chapter 6, the language you use can have significant impact on how well you deal with life issues. For example, when people use catastrophic language, it can actually increase their anxiety. Similarly, labeling yourself an "idiot" or calling yourself some other name can make you feel bad.

· When people damn themselves or others, they often use such derogatory labels. These labels have what has sometimes been called *emotive meaning* in contrast to *cognitive meaning* (Copi and Cohen 1998). When you say that the sky is blue, you describe what the sky looks like. This statement has cognitive meaning because it gives you some information about the sky, namely its color. On the other hand, if you say that the sky is beautiful, you do more than describe it. You commend it. This statement has emotive meaning because you express a favorable attitude toward viewing the sky. Conversely, in calling the sky ugly, you express a negative attitude toward viewing the sky. The statement "The sky is ugly" therefore has negative emotive meaning.

Likewise, in calling a person "an idiot," you express a negative attitude toward associating with this person. In fact, it is not uncommon for people to call others derogatory names before treating them inhumanely (Bandura 1990). If someone is "trash," then it is presumably okay to "take it out." This is also why soldiers are typically taught to view "the enemy" as less than human. Thus, the term "clearing the field" is sometimes used in military combat to refer to destroying the enemy, whereas the death of innocent civilians is labeled "collateral damage." Here, killing other people is framed in dehumanizing terms so that the mission is more easily accomplished than if these deaths were framed in terms of human casualties.

So what happens when you apply derogatory labels to yourself? In effect, you are telling yourself not to associate with yourself. What this means, in practical terms, is that you are giving up on or condemning yourself. However, you have seen that people are not like worn-out shoes to be thrown out. Instead, people are centers of unconditional, inherent value and dignity. You can therefore condemn your actions, but you cannot and should not condemn yourself. This means that it is inappropriate for you to apply derogatory labels to yourself. It's okay for you to say that what you did was stupid, but from this, you cannot correctly infer that *you* are stupid.

Accordingly, you should avoid applying derogatory labels to yourself and generally avoid applying them to anyone. Just as you are not a proper subject of such labels, neither is anyone else, and if you are in a habit of applying these labels to others, it is easier to apply them to yourself. So, as an antidote to self-damnation, you would avoid applying derogatory labels to yourself as well as to anyone else.

EXERCISE: Avoid Degrading Labels

Do the following:

1. Write down as many degrading labels as you can think of that you tend to use to berate yourself or others.

2. Now take a marker (preferably a red one) and put a big bold X across your entire list to indicate that these words are from now on off-limits as labels for people, yourself included.

3. In the future, if and when you feel inclined to call yourself or another by any of the labels on your list, visualize the big bold X you have placed across it.

Stop Second-Guessing Your Ability to Deal with the Task at Hand

Dutiful worriers often fear making mistakes and make their self-worth contingent on not making them. But making mistakes is human. The idea that you are unworthy if you make a mistake is therefore easily refuted, for if it were true, then everyone would be unworthy since everyone makes mistakes. So making mistakes is an inevitable part of life. Not only are mistakes inevitable, but, of course, we can also learn from them.

• Jim's Story

A former client named Jim worked as a psychiatric nurse in an in-patient facility. He told himself that he always had to be in control because his patients' lives depended on him, and that if anything untoward happened on his watch, it would be his fault and he would be a worthless person. As a result, every evening Jim suffered intense anxiety about going to work the next day.

Jim's fear of making a mistake was counterproductive, to say the least. He suffered insomnia each night and was consequently not as alert on the job as he might have been had he gotten a decent night's sleep. But even more important, his conscious life was a steady, painful stream of worrying. So the problem was not Jim's making a mistake. Rather it was his fear of making a mistake.

Epictetus (2009) once asked another man whether, if he were mounted on a horse and well-practiced at combat, he would be anxious about being matched against someone who was not practiced and was merely on foot. To which the other man responded yes, because the person would still have the power to kill him. To which Epictetus responded, then go and sit in a corner and live unhappily without doing anything constructive. Clearly, you cannot live a happy, productive life if you lack confidence.

True, being overconfident is a vice, as when people have a false sense of confidence about handling a task at hand. On the other hand, there is also a vice in under-confidence, which is the tendency of most dutiful worriers. Jim's dutiful worrying was a case in point. Jim had been trained as a psychiatric nurse, and he was competent at what he did. So there was no reason for him to question his ability to handle the matters that confronted him in his professional life. Was there a guarantee that he would not make a mistake? Of course not. But mistakes are part of the price of living.

Once Jim learned to deal with his fear of making a mistake, his life improved. It turned out that Jim's fear of making mistakes was rooted in his demand for approval. In fact, his overwhelming demand for control at work was due to his demand to sustain the approval of his supervisor. If he messed up, he feared this approval would be withdrawn, and he would then be an unworthy or bad person. So his life was filled with intense worry about making mistakes.

It was not until Jim began to work on his demand for approval that his life improved. Jim had to reframe his idea that his self-worth depended on what others thought of him. He had to learn to take reasonable risks (in both his professional and private life) to do what he thought was appropriate, without worrying about how others might perceive his actions. As a result, he became more confident and less afraid of making mistakes.

If the possibility of making a mistake is something you fear, then you have set yourself up for needless worry. It would be better to reframe the possibility of making a mistake as the inevitable price of living a happy and productive life. That is, without taking any risks, you will not act, and unless you act, you will not successfully manage your situation or achieve your goals. And if you do happen to make a mistake, you are not to be damned, for you are, after all, only human.

You might think: *But how do I know when I am just being overconfident about my ability to handle a situation?* This is a question with which many dutiful worriers struggle. In Jim's case, he had professional training, but many challenges in life do not come complete with a course of study and a list of skills to be mastered. For example, what does it take to be a competent mom?

If you are a mom and you care about your children, and have managed to feed, clothe, shelter, and establish a general rapport with them and they with you, then you are likely tuned into their welfare, interests, and needs. From the inception of humankind, moms have cared for their children, and the human race has managed to survive. So you would have good reason to think that you are up for the task of motherhood.

Again, whatever your situation, if you are a dutiful worrier, you have placed yourself under an unnecessary burden of stress. It is the fear of making mistakes and not the actual making of mistakes that is your primary problem. As an antidote to dutiful worrying, you can stop second-guessing your ability to deal with the task at hand.

EXERCISE: Reframe Your Thinking About Making Mistakes

In the following statement, see if you can fill in the blank with a task about which you are or have been afraid of making a mistake:

If I make a mistake at doing _____,
then my rating of my self-worth is diminished.

Now ask yourself, are you at least as competent at this task as the average person in your situation? Be objective: before answering this question, consider evidence such as your experience, degree of commitment, and training (if applicable). Remember too that everybody makes mistakes.

If your answer is yes, that you are at least as competent at this task as the average person in your situation, then tell yourself to stop second-guessing yourself. It's absurd to demand absolute certainty that you won't make a mistake. If your answer is no, that you are not as competent at this task as the average person in your situation, then remind yourself that your self-worth is independent of how well you perform this task.

Now, ask yourself if the task is one from which you could learn, even if you did make a mistake. If so, then think of the possibility of making a mistake as an opportunity to learn and grow. Can the task at hand be useful or beneficial? If so, then think of the risk of making a mistake in performing it as a condition of doing something useful or beneficial.

You can stop your dutiful worrying by giving up the irrational idea that you would somehow be less of a person if you made a mistake. The next time you begin to dutifully worry about possibly making a mistake, reframe the possibility of making a mistake as an unavoidable part of living a happy and productive life, and stop second-guessing your ability to handle your situation.

Love Yourself As Your Own Best Friend

Unconditional self-respect means finding the golden mean between vanity and self-abasement (see chapter 5). That is, the unconditionally self-accepting person neither inflates his abilities nor damns himself for failing to accomplish a certain goal. Because he sees his self-worth as unconditional, he sees his failures as opportunities to learn and do better in the future.

As Aristotle maintained, such a person is his own best friend. Your best friend, according to Aristotle (1941), is someone who wishes you well for your own sake, and not for something in return, and this description of a best friend can be found in a person's attitude toward himself.

Indeed, the person who has unconditional self-respect wishes himself well for his own sake and is therefore his own best friend. Yet he does not demand more than what he deserves. For example, he does not expect others to make special exceptions for him, such as paying him more than anyone else for the same quality work or granting him special honors that he has not earned.

This is in contrast to a self-abasing person who does not wish herself well at all. It is also in contrast to a vain person who wishes herself well but does so by attempting to deceive herself or others into thinking she has accomplished more than she has. This person does not have unconditional self-respect, because she still perceives her self-worth in terms of her accomplishments, albeit in terms of a false sense of these accomplishments.

So, if you have unconditional self-respect, you will love yourself as your own best friend. That is, you will wish yourself well without attempting to deceive yourself or others about your accomplishments and without attempting to use your accomplishments, the approval of others, or other such provisos as a basis for wishing (or not wishing) yourself well.

Dutiful worriers do not treat themselves as their own best friends, because they subject themselves to needless, protracted stress; debase themselves; and deny their self-worth on the basis of their mistakes and lack of approval from others. If this describes you, then you need to change your self-abasing attitude and unconditionally, without any strings attached, wish yourself well.

You may ask, "But wouldn't loving myself as my own best friend make me selfish?" On the contrary, being selfish involves being inconsiderate of others, whereas loving yourself as your own best friend involves just the opposite. In fact, you can't realistically hope to be anyone else's best friend if you are not first and foremost your own best friend. Indeed, while you are stressing yourself out, you are also creating an environment of nervous tension for others who come in contact with you. It is self-defeating to worry about the well-being of others while at the same time creating a stressful environment for them. Love yourself as your own best friend, and you'll be a better friend to others too.

EXERCISE: Treat Yourself As Your Own Best Friend

Ask yourself if you love yourself as your own best friend. Make a list of examples that support your answer. For example, do you ever look for reasons to berate yourself, such as having made a mistake? Do you play blame games with yourself in order to berate yourself? As examples, feel free to refer to your responses to some of the other exercises earlier in this chapter.

Does the list of examples you have just generated suggest that you do not love yourself as your own best friend? If so, then it's time to rethink your view of yourself. Resolve that you are not going to do the things that you've listed but instead will love yourself as your own best friend.

Applying the Antidotes to Self-Damnation

The cognitive antidotes to self-damnation that were presented in this chapter are useful tools for attaining the moral virtue of unconditional self-respect. They are therefore an essential ingredient in overcoming dutiful worrying, for people who unconditionally respect themselves can remind themselves that their self-worth is not contingent on their worrying. Accordingly, the following exercise will show you how to apply these antidotes in the context of going through the four-step process for overcoming dutiful worrying. You should do this exercise whenever you start to tell yourself that you would be a bad person if you allowed a feared prospect (your worry chain) to happen.

EXERCISE: Build Unconditional Self-Respect

Take each of the following steps to overcome self-damnation and build unconditional self-respect.

Step 1: Identify your faulty reasoning. First, find your worry chain. Remember to ask yourself what you are worried about. And then ask yourself why you are worried about it until you have constructed your full worry chain. Remember that the chain ends with something that you are worried about for its own sake.

After you have articulated your worry chain, identify your dutiful-worrying reasoning, using the following template to express your two premises and conclusion:

1. "If I don't keep worrying about [insert first link here], I won't be able to control things and [insert last link here] might happen." (losing-control anxiety)

2. Then I'd be a bad person for having let [insert last link here] happen." (self-damnation)

3. "So, I have to keep worrying about [insert first link here] until I'm certain I've found the best solution to it." (dutiful perfectionism)

As indicated above, take each of the blank spaces in the template to refer to the first and last links in the worry chain you just constructed and play out the resulting reasoning in your mind. That is, say it quietly to yourself.

Step 2: Refute the fallacies in your thinking. Use the following checklist to refute the fallacies in the second premise of your dutiful-worrying reasoning.

☐ You have double standards, rating yourself as bad (worthless or a failure) but not applying the same standards to everyone else.

☐ You are confusing the deed with the doer by rating yourself rather than your deed.

☐ You are telling yourself that if you're not perfect then you're worthless.

Recall that by checking off any item on this list, you have satisfactorily refuted your self-damnation, as you have shown yourself exactly what is wrong with it.

Step 3: Take a rational approach. To build unconditional self-respect, find some cognitive antidotes to your self-damnation. Choose two or more cognitive antidotes from among those presented in this chapter and apply these antidotes to your worry. For example, you may want to ask yourself if you have been treating yourself as an object by degrading yourself and then rehearse the distinction you have learned between an object and a person. Or if you have been calling yourself degrading names, you would tell yourself to stop using them. If necessary, review the previous exercises in this chapter to choose and implement a suitable antidote. After you have done these cognitive exercises, give yourself a behavioral assignment to do something that you enjoy doing.

Step 4: Use your willpower muscle to stop worrying. Make yourself do your behavioral assignment now (or as soon as you can) even if you don't feel like doing it. If you start to feel guilty, repeat step 2 and apply and follow your selected antidotes. Focus your attention on doing your behavioral assignment and enjoy yourself!

After you have completed this exercise, congratulate yourself for having taken yet another major positive step toward overcoming your dutiful worrying. You deserve to feel good about it.

This last exercise has given you an opportunity to work on building unconditional self-respect. Completing this exercise is therefore another milestone in working on overcoming your dutiful worrying.

Again, try not to demand perfection. You will keep improving with practice, but you will always be human, so give yourself permission to make mistakes. This is part of the process of learning and growing.

The next chapter will again give you an opportunity to work on the four-step process, focusing on some antidotes to dutiful perfectionism to help you develop realistic expectations and the moral virtue of serenity.

CHAPTER 8

Attaining Serenity in an Imperfect World

When people engage in dutiful worrying, they think they must keep disturbing themselves about a perceived problem until they are sure they have found the perfect (or near-perfect) solution. Such self-instruction involves a demand for certainty about having found this perfect solution: *Well, maybe there's a better solution, so I must keep thinking about it until I have found it.*

Of course, the world is not a perfect place, nor is it a place that allows for certainty. So, if you are making such demands for perfection and certainty, you are trying to attain something that is, by its very nature, unattainable, and that keeps you in limbo.

Letting go of this demand may be difficult, however. Not infrequently, dutiful worriers are dealing with concerns about loved ones, and they simply don't want to take any chances whatsoever that something very bad might happen to them.

Perhaps you think: *So maybe I shouldn't stop my dutiful worrying if it means putting my loved ones in jeopardy.* Again, the reality is that you will never find the perfect solution to your perceived problem, no matter how much you worry, and you will never eliminate all risks of something undesirable happening, no matter how hard you try.

You may think: *But even if I don't eliminate all risks, the more I worry, maybe I can eliminate most of them or at least do my best.* In fact, it is more likely that excessive worrying will have the opposite effect, for the intense stress brought about by worrying is likely to adversely affect your cognition and memory. So, again, engaging in dutiful worrying is likely to defeat your very purpose.

Overcoming Your Dutiful Perfectionism

Accordingly, it is now time to work on giving up the self-defeating, dutiful perfectionism that keeps you in a suspended state of dutiful worrying. This chapter introduces some useful antidotes to this unrealistic demand, which will, in turn, help you to attain the moral virtue of serenity. Remember that serenity is the golden mean between demanding perfection, on the one hand, and indifference to how things are, on the other hand. It means being comfortable with living in an imperfect world.

Having serenity means having realistic expectations. This means accepting the fact that the world is not a perfect place, that human beings are fallible creatures, that the future is inherently probabilistic and uncertain, and that not everything is foreseeable and within your control. Having serenity means that you will be in a habit of realistically and rationally confronting these realities.

Having realistic expectations makes it easier to approach moral problems. Without serenity, you are less likely to make rational moral choices. For example, if you demand certainty before you do anything, you are likely to make decisions by indecision; that is, you will not act at all and then will bear the consequences of your indecision. Furthermore, many moral problems do not admit of just one clear solution. So if you demand perfection about solving moral problems, you are likely to miss, or dismiss, alternative ways of approaching such problems. Accordingly, this chapter will address how to attain serenity, which will lead the way to more rational moral decision-making (see chapter 9).

Again, demanding perfection is the basis of dutiful perfectionism. That is, if you commit this reasoning fallacy, then you demand certainty, or you demand that your wants, desires, or preferences are always satisfied, or you demand that you perform perfectly. In contrast, in taking a realistic approach to reality, the serene person does not ordinarily make such unrealistic demands.

Some Cognitive Antidotes to Dutiful Perfectionism

So what antidotes to these unrealistic demands can help you to attain serenity? They would include the following:

- Instead of focusing on or looking for what is negative or wrong in the world, think too about what is positive or right in it.

- Instead of procrastinating, accept the limits of what you can know, and be prepared to act on your imperfect knowledge.

- Instead of demanding that the world be perfect, drop the idea of perfection, replace it with an idea of what might be better, and reframe risks as a means to making things better.

- Avoid demanding perfection in setting and attempting to meet your goals.

- Change your absolute, unrealistic musts and shoulds to preferences.

- Be prepared to tolerate disappointment.

By applying these antidotes to your dutiful perfectionism, you can attain serenity in an imperfect world.

Think About What Is Positive or Right in the World

You may look for things to worry about: *Things just seem too good to be true. There just has to be something I'm overlooking that I should be worrying about.* And then you start to feel guilty because you think you still should be making yourself worry about something or other. It is then not very long before you find what you are looking for, that is, something you had not previously been worrying about but, as you now see it, you should have been worrying about: *How am I ever going to pay all these mounting bills if I don't get a raise? And to think I was so naïve as to let myself be happy when they told me yesterday that I would be getting it. Maybe they'll change their minds or even fire me instead!*

Indeed, it is possible for negative, unanticipated things to happen to you and your loved ones. It's possible that a brushfire will spontaneously ignite and burn your house down. But looking for such things to worry about is not only unproductive; it is a source of needless stress. It is far better to think about the good things in your life. This does not mean that you should tell yourself that everything is terrific and that your life is absolutely perfect. This extreme can also be self-defeating.

In fact, if you think that everything's perfect, then you may end up thinking that things are absolutely awful when something undesirable happens. So you don't want to whitewash and misrepresent reality. Still, there are also truly good things to think about or to be thankful for that you may now be taking for granted. A good example might be your health. It's easy enough for people who are not normally in severe pain to fail to appreciate the absence of pain.

I can recall the time I had kidney stones. It is sometimes said that this sort of pain is as intense as giving birth. Certainly it must be less rewarding. The passing of my kidney stone was the most excruciating pain I had ever endured. Not even pain pills were capable of taking the edge off of it, and during this experience, I would have been grateful for just a few moments of pain-free existence.

Since then, I do sometime think of how good it feels to be pain free. Doing so is a good thing. And certainly it's better to focus on feeling good about your health rather than worrying about it. So if you're relatively healthy, feel good about it.

On the other hand, perhaps you are not now relatively pain free. Maybe you have arthritis or some other painful chronic illness. Or maybe you have diabetes, which is potentially dangerous if not controlled. So should you spend your waking hours worrying about it? Do you have a duty to worry about your condition?

The answer is no. It makes a lot more sense to manage your disease and to move on with your life. Remaining in a suspended state of worrying is counterproductive. It only makes you feel worse. Better to set your mind on things that are positive and beneficial than to get bogged down in negativity. If you look at the world as a battlefield in which you must constantly be on your guard, you will be that way.

Remembering what is good in your life does not mean that you should ignore what's bad, but there is a difference between managing problems and obsessing over them so that they occupy the greater part of your life. Unfortunately, if you are a dutiful worrier, then you tend to get bogged down in the negative stuff and find less satisfaction out of living than you could.

So the key is to work on your problems but use rational restraint. When you are inclined to focus on what's wrong or to look for such things, treat this inclination with this constructive antidote: tell yourself to also think about what's positive.

EXERCISE: Think About the Positive

Do the following:

1. Ask yourself if you tend to unnecessarily focus on or look for what is negative or wrong in the world. Do you do this at least some of the time? If so, record a few examples of such negative things that you have focused on and unnecessarily stressed yourself over.

2. Make a list of as many things that you can think of that are positive in the world, including things in your own life and the lives of loved ones. Pay special attention to what you might have been taking for granted, but also list what you have already acknowledged as positive. Consider this list a

work-in-progress, and feel free to add to it as you think of further items.

The next time you start to focus on or look for what is negative or wrong, take out your list and read it to yourself.

Be Prepared to Act on Your Imperfect Knowledge

In demanding perfect or near-perfect knowledge, dutiful worriers go beyond the limits of what any human being can reasonably expect to know. This demand can be driven by the fear of not knowing enough to control the outcome of a situation. So accepting the limits of your knowledge is important to overcoming the habit of dutiful worrying.

What then are the limits of your knowledge?

First, your knowledge of future events is never certain. If you wait to be certain before acting, you will simply never act. For example, you can decide to stay at your current job instead of looking for another job because you are afraid of making the move in a bad job market and want to play it safe. Still you may end up getting laid off from your current job. There are no guarantees, no matter what you decide to do. So one limitation on your knowledge about the future is that it is never certain. Living in the world means accepting some measure of risk.

This doesn't mean you can't have a reasonable belief about the future. Indeed you can. Thus, other things being equal, it is more reasonable to believe that you have a greater chance of landing a job for which you are qualified than one for which you are unqualified. But guarantees are not part of the fabric of the real world, so it is self-defeating to insist on them before acting.

The second limit on your knowledge is that you cannot solve a contradiction. For example, a thirty-four-year-old woman named Jackie once told me that she wanted to find someone, settle down, and have children. Yet she also told me that she really was not ready to settle down.

• Jackie's Story

Jackie had spent several months ruminating over her perceived problem in search of a solution. Unfortunately, she didn't realize that there was, in fact, no possible solution, for what she wanted to do was to both settle down and not settle down, which was impossible.

The kind of thinking that led Jackie to embrace contradictory paths is known as *dilemma thinking*. This is the kind of thinking that people do when they think that they are "caught between a rock and a hard place" or "damned if you do and damned if you don't." Here's what Jackie thought: *Either I settle down and raise a family or I don't. If I settle down, I'll have to give up my freedom and won't be able to do all the things that I enjoy doing as a single adult. On the other hand, if I don't settle down, then I won't have the chance to have kids. So neither option is going to work for me.* Indeed, Jackie wanted it both ways, but she simply couldn't have it both ways.

Often, when people generate such contradictions through dilemma thinking, it is because they have mixed emotions. But as long as you are afraid to take a risk and to make a commitment to one scenario or another, you will remain in limbo for a long time, and your decision will be made for you as a result of changes beyond your control. For example, if she procrastinated for too long, Jackie would eventually not be able to conceive.

The real challenge for Jackie was that she was afraid to give up something—her independent single status, on the one hand, or her opportunity to raise a family, on the other. You may also notice that Jackie's dilemma thinking was part of her problem because it kept her ruminating and vacillating over the unsavory consequences of each of her options, which interfered with her choosing either option.

Such thinking will be examined in greater detail in chapter 10.

The third limit on your knowledge is simply that you can't know everything. Indeed, the more you learn, the more you will find out how much you really don't know. Can you recall how simple things seemed when you were a small child? Indeed, it is a mark of maturity to realize that there are many things that you don't know. This point was expressed by the ancient thinker Socrates, once said by a prophet to be the wisest man in Athens. Socrates interpreted the prophet's claim to mean that he above all others knew just how little he really knew. Such humility gave Socrates a good name among his peers, for he was not disposed to pass on false information or to react in ill-advised ways. Indeed, his quest for knowledge often ended with the realization that he simply did not know.

Like Socrates, you should be open to the fact that there are things, indeed many things, you don't know. It can be helpful to look upon your knowledge of what you don't know, not as a failure on your part but, instead, as a mark of wisdom: *Okay, so there are many things I don't know. But whoever said I had a duty to know everything? At least I'm wise enough to know the limits of my own knowledge.*

Even if you don't know everything, you can act on what you do know. This means accepting the fact that no matter how long and hard you persist in your search for wisdom, there will always be things you won't know. It also means drawing the line where you have expended a reasonable effort, not where you have reached the bottom of the well of knowledge. For you will never reach that point.

Instead, you simply need to give yourself permission to act: *Okay, I can keep ruminating about what to do, trying to find out more and more about my situation. But at some point, I am going to have to make a decision anyway, and there will still be things I won't know. So I am not going to agonize over this situation. I am just going to do a reasonably thorough job and then act. After all, I am not a perfect being with infinite wisdom like God. I am a human being, which means my knowledge is always going to be finite and imperfect.*

So you should accept the limitations on your knowledge and be prepared to act. Otherwise, you will remain in limbo, causing you as well as others unnecessary stress.

EXERCISE: Appreciate the Limits of Your Knowledge

It is one thing to tell yourself that you don't have to be certain before acting and another to translate this self-talk into action. Try the following behavioral assignments:

1. Consider something that you are not certain about but nevertheless have a reasonable belief that you are right about it. Then act on it. For example, perhaps you are not sure if your significant other will like the present you have considered giving him. Still, you have a reasonable belief that he may like it. Instead of procrastinating about it, give it to him. Even if it turns out that he's not enthralled with the gift, congratulate yourself for not having sat around worrying about whether he would like it.

2. Have you ever painted yourself into a corner by defining your problem in terms of a contradiction that cannot be solved? See if you can come up with an example or two.

3. Do you tend to set reasonable limits on the amount of knowledge you require to make a decision, or do you keep telling yourself that you have to have more and more information, without limit, before making a decision about it? Provide at least one example that illustrates the way you usually approach acquiring knowledge to solve problems.

4. Do you sometimes see your lack of knowledge as a failure on your part? Do you condemn yourself for being ignorant and demand that you remedy the defect? See if you can think of a situation where you've done this. For example, perhaps you have found out how much you really don't know about parenting and have viewed this as a failure on your part. Now, see if you can reframe this situation as a positive, learning experience.

Reframe Risks As a Means to Make Things Better

There is an important difference between demanding perfection and trying to improve or make things better. When you demand perfection, you set yourself up for failure, for you will never achieve it in this imperfect world. However, if you strive to make things better, you can actually meet your mark.

Consider that a perfect world is not even desirable, for if things were perfect, then there would be no room for advancement. As William James expressed, "Freedom in a world already perfect could only mean freedom to be *worse*, and who could be so insane as to wish that?...Surely the only *possibility* that one can rationally claim is the possibility that things may be *better*" (1995, 85).

Imagine a perfect world. This would presumably be a world in which there were no dangers and hence no risks in choosing one thing instead of another. It might seem like paradise at first, but would it really be paradise? In such a perfect universe, there would be no courageous feats because there would be no risks; no great medical discoveries and hence no point to studying medicine because there would be no diseases; no need to learn from experience because no ill would ever come to anyone; no prudent acts because imprudence would not matter. In a perfect world, there would be no mistakes to be made, but there would be no place to progress either.

Such a perfect world would be perfectly boring! It would be a world in which there would be nothing to look forward to. That is, without the possibility of disappointment, the prospect of attaining something of worth would be meaningless. Success would be meaningless if there weren't also the possibility of failure.

So, paradoxically, there may be good reason to celebrate the fact that the world is imperfect. Instead of demanding perfection, it is thus more rational to replace your idea of trying to achieve perfection with the idea of making things better. Things can always get better, so there can always be something to aim for. This is less boring, and it leaves open the meaningfulness of cultivating virtue, taking risks, and confronting danger. Instead of worrying about risks and dangers as though they were the stuff of an evil universe, you can reframe them as the necessary baggage of a world full of interesting challenges and opportunities for making things better and better.

EXERCISE: Replace "Perfect" with "Better"

Take the following steps to replace your idea of trying to achieve perfection with the idea of making things better:

1.   Get out your pen or pencil and write down a list of things that you would like to do in your lifetime that you think would make the world a better place.

2.   Look at each entry on this list and cross through each entry that would involve taking risks or overcoming dangers.

3.   How many things are left on your list of things to do?

4.   Now imagine that the world was perfect so that everything on your original list of things to do would have already been done. Which world would you prefer to live in, the perfect world or the present one? Why?

5.   In light of what you've discovered in this exercise, fill in the blank in the following statement with the word "better" or the word "perfect":

     I prefer that the world be a _____ place.

Avoid Demanding Perfection in Reaching Your Goals

Dutiful worriers invariably demand perfection about attaining the goals they set for themselves. For example, demanding that you be certain that bad things won't happen is such a perfectionistic demand. Telling yourself that you must never make a mistake is also such a perfectionistic demand. So too is demanding that things always go the way you want them to go, and so too is demanding that you control things that are not in your power to control. All of these are demands that many dutiful worriers often make of themselves.

It is generally not the particular goals that you set that creates unnecessary stress but rather the demand that you make on yourself to achieve them. For example, I know someone who loves to perform and hopes someday to be on Broadway. Statistically, the odds of achieving this goal are low, given the relatively few roles available and the incredible amount of competition among many talented actors, but there is no harm in my friend hoping that she makes it to Broadway.

You might be an actor in community theater with big ambitions. The problem arises when you transmute a hope, wish, or desire into a demand that you achieve an unlikely goal: *I must be on Broadway. I am meant to be on Broadway, and I cannot and will not have it any other way. Unless I am on Broadway, anything else I do in my life is simply second-rate and unworthy of me and my talents.*

This demand is what creates the stress. Indeed, the problem is not with aiming high. You can shoot for the stars. There is nothing wrong with it. But if you *demand* that you reach the stars, then you have put undue stress on yourself.

In fact, it can be constructive to set idealistic goals even if you know you aren't likely to reach them. For example, I know someone who wants to write the great American novel and to be as celebrated as John Steinbeck and Ernest Hemingway, but he is realistic enough to know that he probably won't attain this goal. Still, he has a couple of novels now in the oven on a slow bake and is motivated to complete them because he has a goal in view. Of course, he knows that if he is fortunate enough, maybe one of these novels will see the light of day. But he can still hope that one of his novels really will catapult him to stardom. Is it likely? No. But great things can happen when people have dreams.

Just look at Barack Obama. When he was in the fourth grade and the students were going around the classroom saying what they wanted to be when they grew up, Obama got up and said he wanted to be president of the United States. This was his dream. Given the odds of becoming president, let alone the first black president, Obama's dream was highly unlikely to come true. But it did.

So it can be a good thing to dream and to have high aspirations, just as long as you don't demand that you attain them. If you do attain them, then that's well and good. If you don't, then that's okay too.

In fact, even if you don't attain your dreams, they can get you started on a path that may ultimately lead you to another place where you can be quite comfortable. One intriguing aspect about goal setting is that in aiming at one goal, you may forge another goal, and in aiming at that goal, you may forge yet another goal, and then another, and then still another, and so on. This is exciting because you do not know exactly where you will end up. So instead of seeing your present goals and aspirations as carved in stone, it would be more realistic to reframe them as tentative and subject to change as you journey through life and come upon more opportunities.

As you reframe your goals as tentative and subject to change, you will attain greater serenity. Please also remember that giving up the demand for perfection includes not demanding that you be perfect in your effort to give it up. In fact, many dutiful worriers on their way to recovery go through a stage where they make this demand on themselves: I'm supposed to be making progress, so I'm not supposed to be demanding perfection at this stage. So why did I just demand perfection?

If you catch yourself doing this, you can treat it like any other case of demanding perfection. Tell yourself that you don't have to be perfect, and give yourself permission to make mistakes: *Yes, my goal is to overcome demanding perfection, but that doesn't mean I have to be perfect in attaining this goal. It's okay to mess up. After all, I'm only human.*

So you can shoot for the stars. Those great goals, aspirations, and dreams can sometimes come true. And even if they don't, they can inspire you to act and thus help you carve out other goals as you live your life. This can be an exciting adventure, a story written as you go along. Hold on to your dreams, but don't demand that they come true.

EXERCISE: Reframe Your Goals Without Demanding Perfection

Take the following steps to reframe your goals:

1. Make a list of some of the things you want to accomplish in your lifetime.

2.　Ask yourself if any of the items on your list are things that you believe you must accomplish in your lifetime. Are you stressing yourself out about the possibility of not accomplishing these things?

3.　Now ask yourself if you have ever discovered a new interest or talent as a result of doing something else. For example, perhaps you had a job that you may not have even wanted at first but then discovered that you enjoyed or discovered that you had a talent for some aspect of this work. Does the possibility of making such accidental discoveries help you to be more open minded about the possibility of setting new, different goals for the future?

4.　Now make a list of things that you have already accomplished in your life that you regard as positive. Are there any past accomplishments on this list that have influenced your current goals? For example, some people do unexpectedly well in a college course and, as a result, decide to go into a related field.

5.　From looking at your past experiences, can you see how your current goals could also be modified or changed?

Based on this exercise, can you say that you are a work-in-progress and that therefore it is unreasonable to make demands on yourself about goals that may well change as you discover or cultivate new interests or talents? Try reframing as tentative and subject to change any current goal you think you must accomplish.

Change Your Musts and Shoulds to Preferences

Demands for perfection are typically cast in the language of "must" and "should" or their synonyms (like "have to" and "ought"). Thus you think: *I must always get what I want. I should always be able to control things. People should never treat me unfairly. I must always do a perfect job.* This thought process locks you in to a stressful roller coaster ride through life, for when you think that things are not turning out the way you say they must or should be, then you will feel stressed. And if you tell yourself that you are responsible for what must or should be, then you will feel guilty.

The language in question is *absolutistic*. This means that it refers to an unconditional demand, or to a must or should that is always binding. Terms such as "must always" or "must never" are prototypes of such absolutistic language.

Absolutistic musts and shoulds may be sometimes confused with conditional ones. For example, the statement "If you want to be healthy, then you must [or should] eat healthy food" asserts a conditional (as distinct from an unconditional) must. The must here is dependent on whether or not you want to be healthy. This conditional "must" asserts a means-end connection between eating healthy foods (the means) and being healthy (the end).

Dutiful worriers tend to make unconditional demands by using absolutistic musts, shoulds, or their equivalents. But they also use these in combination with conditional musts or shoulds: I must worry until I am certain about what to do. And I must be certain about what to do. Here you assert (or imply) the means-end connection between worrying and being certain. That is, you think that if you keep worrying enough, then you will eventually be certain about what to do. However, you also include an unconditional must, because you say (or imply) that you must be certain about what to do. This latter "must" makes a demand for perfection because it is unrealistic and perfectionistic to demand certainty in an imperfect world.

The conditional must that's implied between worrying and certainty is easily shown to be false because it's clear that no matter how much you worry, you cannot attain certainty. In other words, unlike eating healthy foods as a means to good health, worrying cannot serve as a means to certainty. In fact, worrying is self-defeating because it creates stress, which makes it harder to think rationally. As you will see in chapter 9, there are more rational ways than worrying to address your problems.

The unconditional must (that you must be certain) is also unrealistic for the same reason, namely that it supposes that you can have certainty in the first place, which is false. On the other hand, you might *prefer* to have certainty if indeed you could have it. So you could reasonably replace "must be" with "would prefer that": *Yes, I would prefer that I be certain, but I realize that it would be unrealistic and futile to demand that I have certainty.*

Notice the difference between saying, "I would prefer to be certain, but I don't have to be certain" and saying, "I must be certain." The first statement removes the stressful demand for perfection. It is inconsistent with worrying. So a useful antidote for deflating and redirecting absolutistic perfectionistic "musts" is to change them to preferences.

Thus, you can reasonably assert: *I would prefer to always get what I want. I would prefer to always be able to control things. I would prefer that people never treat me unfairly. I would prefer to always do a perfect job.* While you can rationally prefer these things, you cannot rationally demand that you must have them.

EXERCISE: Change Your Perfectionistic Musts and Shoulds to Preferences

The following are some common absolutistic (unconditional) perfectionistic musts. Check off any and all that you have applied to yourself:

- ☐ You must always have the approval of others, or at least of certain people.

- ☐ You must always perform perfectly and never make a mistake.

- ☐ You must always be certain of things before you make a decision.

- ☐ You must always find something to worry about.

- ☐ You must always find a perfect or near-perfect solution to your (important) problems.

- ☐ You must always have things go the way you want.

- ☐ You must always be treated fairly.

- ☐ You must never have bad things happen to you or to your loved ones.

- ☐ You must always be in control, or at least in control of whatever you think is important.

☐ You must always get what you want.

☐ You must never fail at anything, or at least at anything you think is important.

☐ You must always look perfect or near-perfect.

Now, for each statement you have checked off, cross through the words "must always" or "must never." Then rewrite each of these statements, replacing the words you crossed through with the expression "would prefer that you," turning these statements about what you must experience into expressions of what you would prefer.

After rewriting your musts and shoulds as preferences, quietly repeat aloud each of the new statements you just created.

You can do this exercise whenever you start to tell yourself that you must or should do something. Converting the "must" to a preference and then repeating the converted statement quietly to yourself will help you cultivate the virtue of serenity.

Be Prepared to Tolerate Disappointment

When you change your "musts" to preferences, you are committing yourself to being prepared to have your preferences not always satisfied. This means that you are committing yourself to being disappointed sometimes. So you should accordingly be prepared to tolerate disappointment.

Indeed, since preferences for such things as certainty, full control, how others should always treat you, getting everything you want, and so forth are unlikely to come your way, you may as well be prepared for disappointment. So what can you say to yourself when you don't get what you want? *Okay, so I would have preferred to have gotten what I wanted, but that's just not always the way it goes. I am not always going to have it my way. That's just being unrealistic.* In so saying, you will have given yourself reason to tolerate disappointment.

Such tolerance is an important part of the virtue of serenity, which implies that you do not fall to pieces when you don't get what you prefer. However, this does not mean that you can't be disappointed at all: *Of course, I'm disappointed that I didn't get the job even though I thought I was more qualified than the other candidates, but that doesn't mean I should make myself crazy about it. After all, not everything in this world is fair, so I need to be prepared for these sorts of things.*

Such tolerance is at the root of being able to succeed. If you are not prepared for disappointment, then you may never strive for success. If you don't risk failing, then you won't ever succeed. But should you always be tolerant? For example, if you think you have been unfairly treated, then, instead of simply accepting it, shouldn't you fight back?

Ideally, every iniquity should indeed be redressed. However, in the real world, not every battle needs to be waged and not every cause is worth it. You should therefore choose your battles wisely. Some of them may be worthwhile whereas others may just be a waste of time, effort, and resources. So the golden mean applies here as elsewhere. One extreme is to have a combatant attitude with an inclination to overreact and do battle whenever you think you have been wronged. The other extreme is to be docile and easily taken advantage of. The golden mean lies somewhere between these two extremes and involves knowing which causes to take up and which to leave alone. This is a challenge for all of us, but it requires that you be prepared to tolerate disappointment. Otherwise, you will tend to go to the extreme of overreacting and miss attaining the golden mean.

EXERCISE: Learn to Tolerate Disappointment

Do the following:

1. Review the previous exercise and select the "must" that you think creates the most stress for you.

2. Write down what you usually say to yourself when this must is not met. For example, if you said that you must have the approval of others, what do you tell yourself when the others in question disapprove of you?

3. Now, applying what you have learned about tolerating disappointment, reframe your usual response to not having your

must met. For example, suppose you don't get the approval of someone whose approval you demand. What would you say to yourself instead of your usual stress-inducing response?

4. Choose another one of the musts on your list and repeat steps 2 and 3 of this exercise.

Feel free to repeat this exercise. The more practice you get at tolerating disappointment, the better.

Applying the Antidotes to Dutiful Perfectionism

You have now learned some useful antidotes to dutiful perfectionism, which can help you to overcome your reliance on absolutistic musts and shoulds and attain serenity in this imperfect world. Accordingly, the following exercise will show you how to apply these antidotes in the context of going through the four-step process for overcoming dutiful worrying.

EXERCISE: Cultivate Serenity

Take each of the following steps to overcome dutiful perfectionism and to cultivate serenity.

Step 1: Identify your faulty reasoning. First, find your worry chain. Remember to ask yourself what you are worried about. And then ask yourself why you are worried about it until you have constructed your full worry chain. Remember that the chain ends with something that you are worried about for its own sake.

After you have articulated your worry chain, identify your dutiful-worrying reasoning, using the following template to express your two premises and conclusion:

1. "If I don't keep worrying about [insert first link here], I won't be able to control things and [insert last link here] might happen." (losing-control anxiety)

2. Then I'd be a bad person for having let [insert last link here] happen." (self-damnation)

3. "So, I have to keep worrying about [insert first link here] until I'm certain I've found the best solution to it." (dutiful perfectionism)

As indicated above, take each of the blank spaces in the template to refer to the first and last links in the worry chain you just constructed and play out the resulting reasoning in your mind. That is, say it quietly to yourself.

Step 2: Refute the fallacies in your thinking. Use the following checklist to refute the fallacies in the conclusion of your dutiful-worrying reasoning.

☐ You are demanding that you be certain in a world in which you can't have certainty.

☐ You are assuming that because you want or prefer something, it must be that way.

☐ You are demanding more than what you can reasonably expect from an imperfect human being such as yourself.

Step 3: Take a rational approach. To build serenity, find some cognitive antidotes to your dutiful perfectionism. Choose two or more cognitive antidotes from among those presented in this chapter and apply these antidotes to your worry. For example, if you have been looking for what is negative or wrong in the world, concentrate on what is positive or right in it. Or if you have been telling yourself that you must be certain or that you must not make a mistake, change these musts to preferences by reminding yourself that while you would prefer to be certain and to not make a mistake, these are not things that you can rationally demand. If necessary, review the previous exercises in this chapter to choose and implement a suitable antidote to your dutiful perfectionism. After you have done these cognitive exercises, give yourself a behavioral assignment to do something that you enjoy doing.

Step 4: Use your willpower muscle to stop worrying. Make yourself do your behavioral assignment now (or as soon as you can) even if you don't feel like doing it. If you start to feel guilty, repeat step 2 and apply and follow your selected antidotes. Focus your attention on doing your behavioral assignment and enjoy yourself!

After you have completed this exercise, congratulate yourself for having taken yet another major positive step toward overcoming your dutiful worrying. Feel good about it.

Where You Are Now

The preceding exercise guided you through some important aspects of all four steps of the process for overcoming dutiful worrying. By now, you have learned how to identify your dutiful worrying reasoning and find and refute the fallacies that sustain it. You have also learned how to cultivate courage, self-respect, and serenity to counter those fallacies. You have made great progress, for most people who engage in dutiful worrying are not even aware of the faulty thinking that generates their stressful life-style; much less do they know how to stop their dutiful worrying without feeling guilty about it.

The more you practice using the tools at your disposal, the more skillful you will become at applying them and the more virtuous you will get. That is, you will find yourself strengthening the habits of exercising courage in confronting your life challenges, maintaining self-respect amid both your successes and failures, and attaining serenity in an imperfect world. At this juncture, you therefore have all the tools that you need to avoid a considerable amount of stress in your life, so long as you continue to cultivate your skills by practicing them.

So are you now ready to stop your dutiful worrying and to live without such needless stress? Or is something still missing? In the past, you felt a sense of urgency to worry and felt guilty when you tried to stop, because you perceived worrying to be your moral duty. Clearly, this was a noble reason for having put yourself through such stress, and it is not difficult to surmise that you will be dissatisfied with giving up your dutiful worrying unless you receive further guidance in how to do what is morally right.

What you have learned thus far can help you to avoid self-defeating styles of thinking that can indeed prevent you from acting morally. In striving to cultivate courage, unconditional self-respect, and serenity, you will be in a far better place to do the right thing. But more needs to be said about how to do the right thing. An important part of the four-step process is making rational moral decisions, and this will be the focus of the next chapter.

CHAPTER 9

Making Moral Decisions

Why do you engage in dutiful worrying? Clearly, you do it because you have a strong moral conscience and you want to do what's right. You are well meaning and self-sacrificing. Unfortunately, all of this worrying has created needless stress for you and for others, since dutiful worrying tends to be counterproductive.

So what should you do instead? After all, you are not merely interested in avoiding stress. You are also deeply motivated to do what is morally right. This can admittedly be a challenge for any of us. For example, how are you going to decide rationally what to do when there doesn't seem to be a clear-cut solution to your problem? What do you do when you are trying to take care of your mother who has Alzheimer's disease, tend to your three kids, and make your already strained marriage work, and when no matter what you do, it seems someone will get hurt?

When you are lost in such a moral quagmire, it is easy enough to lose your perspective and become desperate. So what sort of antidotes can you apply to your dutiful worrying that will provide you with moral guidance in your situation?

Having been in the trenches for many years, helping people like you make moral decisions, I can tell you that there is no formula for making these decisions and you must make these decisions for yourself. No one can make them for you. That said, this chapter offers some guidelines for how to solve problems in a more rational way.

Some Cognitive Antidotes to Dutiful Worrying

Dutiful worriers typically tell themselves that they must engage in dutiful worrying so that they can solve their problems: *I must keep worrying and ruminating about my problem until I am certain that I have found the perfect or (near-perfect) solution.* Unfortunately, all this worrying and ruminating about your perceived problems produces neither certainty nor perfection (see chapter 8). In fact, it typically interferes with your rational thinking and impedes problem solving. At the same time, you want to do what's right. What you need is some alternative wisdom to correct your reliance on dutiful worrying.

The following antidotes to dutiful worrying will give you a more rational way to solve your moral problems. Rather than offer specific solutions, these antidotes are moral guidelines. Together, they will help you to better understand the nature of moral decision-making and so help you to make more constructive decisions:

1. Make beneficent, respectful, and caring decisions.

2. Be prepared to balance competing ethical interests.

3. Reframe your always- and never-acting moral rules to allow for exceptions.

4. Be prepared to tolerate the inherent ambiguity of moral decision-making.

5. Be prepared to have regrets even if you make a rational moral decision.

By following these guidelines and sticking to your four-step plan for overcoming dutiful worrying, you should be in excellent shape—less stressed, less guilt-ridden, and more satisfied that you have rationally handled your problems and performed in a morally competent way.

Make Beneficent, Respectful, and Caring Decisions

There are three main approaches to moral decision-making that have been defended historically: make beneficent decisions; make respectful decisions; make caring decisions. While defenders of each approach have believed that theirs alone was the approach that should be used, most ethicists today believe that the most rational approach is to use all three.

The Principle of Beneficence

The first of these approaches tells you to act in ways that maximize overall welfare. This is sometimes called the *principle of beneficence* (Beauchamp and Childress 2008). It means that you should act to benefit others as well as yourself. This includes doing positive good for others or removing bad things such as pain and suffering. For example, you might decide to tell your friend that her husband is cheating on her, even though you know it might hurt her in the short term, because you think that it would maximize her welfare in the long run. In applying this principle, you should keep in mind that good consequences seldom occur in isolation from bad ones. Thus, it is hurtful to your friend in the short term to learn of her husband's affair, but you intend that there will be overriding positive value to her in the long run if she learns now rather than later. Contrary to dutiful worrying, where you would look for an ideal solution, this approach acknowledges that it's unreasonable to demand that resolutions to your problems include having only good things happen.

Of course, this does not mean that you should intentionally do harm. It is one thing to tolerate an unavoidable harm in order to bring about an overriding good. It is another to intentionally harm someone without regard to an overriding benefit. A precondition of applying the principle of beneficence is therefore that you try to avoid harming others. Thus, the well-known Hippocratic oath warns physicians against doing harm, but quite clearly, in medicine as well as in other domains, we may end up doing harm, however regrettably, because there simply is no reasonable way to avoid it.

So, according to this moral principle, you should ask yourself what the consequences (both positive and negative) are likely to be if you were to act one way or another. Remember, this calculation needs to be done without magnifying risks or catastrophizing. This is why, to apply the principle of beneficence correctly, dutiful worriers need to work on fighting their tendency to engage in losing-control anxiety, which, as you have seen, involves such exaggerations of consequences.

You may ask, "But how do you know when the positive consequences outweigh the negative ones?" There's no formula for this, and it's important to avoid demanding perfection. In some cases, however, deciding when the positives outweigh the negatives won't be difficult. If you are weighing a small inconvenience against preventing a serious injury, then it's usually a no-brainer. In other cases, this decision will require a judgment call. For example, in some medical contexts, the cure may have serious side-effects that could potentially be worse than the illness. In such cases, the patient's choice can be rational, regardless of whether she decides to go with the therapy or not. Sometimes the deciding factor may be how much value this person places in being rid of the illness in question. Some people are willing to take greater therapeutic risks if their illness prevents them from doing things they love to do or from trying to realize their dreams. For example, an athlete might choose to undergo certain risky surgery that a sedentary person would never consider.

The Principle of Respect for Persons

A second approach to making moral decisions involves basing your decisions on whether they are respectful. According to this *principle of respect for persons*, you should act so that you treat people, including yourself, as persons and not objects (Kant 1964). This idea should already be abundantly familiar to you since it is the basis of an important antidote to self-damnation (see chapter 7). It is also an important consideration for making moral decisions.

According to this principle, people have a right to be fully informed before they make their decisions. They also have a right not to be forced, deceived, tricked, lied to, or otherwise manipulated into doing or not doing things. For example, you would violate this principle if you married someone for his money while feigning love for him. Another violation would be operating on a patient without his informed consent or the consent of his legal guardian. Making deceitful promises, scamming others out of their money, cheating on a partner, forced or nonconsensual sex, and lying to someone even for her own good are some commonplace violations.

This principle also applies to the way you treat yourself. Thus, you should also not treat yourself as though you were an object. For example, you should avoid seeing yourself merely as a vehicle for the welfare or happiness of others, such as family members, without recognizing your own independent status as a person. Of course, dutiful worriers often do just the opposite, thus violating this principle while believing they are doing the right thing.

Care-Based Ethics

A third approach to making moral decisions is sometimes called *care-based ethics*. According to this approach, the point of morality and moral decision-making is to preserve interpersonal relations by harmonizing the welfare, interests, and needs of all concerned. This is to be accomplished by having empathetic understanding for each individual's circumstances, problems, and concerns, and the primary motive would be "the wish not to hurt others and the hope that in morality lies a way of solving conflicts so that no one will get hurt" (Gilligan 1993, 65).

At least this is the hope. Realistically, you must realize that it may be impossible to harmonize everybody's conflicting interests. Your goal would be to try your best within reason to preserve and harmonize such competing interests while recognizing that it may be impossible to please everyone.

Empathetically understanding another's situation is essential to caring; however, it does not mean losing your objectivity. As Carl Rogers points out, to have empathetic understanding is "to sense the client's private world, as if it were your own, but without ever losing the as if quality...." (1961, 284). Notice that this means that to have empathetic understanding, it is "as if" you had entered another's subjective world.

That is, you want to avoid getting lost in that world; you need to maintain some degree of distance so that you can remain objective.

While Rogers was speaking to therapists about empathizing with their clients, he intended this definition of empathy to apply to anyone interested in helping others. So, in caring about another person, it is important to avoid getting so involved that you lose your ability to make a rational decision.

It is easy to lose perspective in this way when trying to make decisions that impact loved ones. For example, one mom became so immersed in the subjective world of her child that she found it difficult to act as an adult on her behalf. When other children at school bullied the child, the mom started to lose perspective. One thing led to another and she ended up having a schoolyard shouting match with the parents of these other children. Unfortunately, this mom had gotten too close to the subjective world of her child and was unable to function as an adult guardian.

So, how do you know when you have the right amount of emotional distance? Imagine getting as close as you can to the edge of a canyon in order to experience the breathtaking view. The key to soaking up the view to its fullest extent is to stop just before you are about to fall off the edge. When you empathize, you will want to get as close as you can to the subjective world of the other without falling into it. If you can do this, you will be able to care for the other person without getting carried away to the point that you impair your ability to make moral decisions.

Morality and Dutiful Worrying

Not one of the three approaches to moral decision-making just discussed can be used to defend a duty to worry. You cannot defend such a duty by appealing to the principle of beneficence, for dutiful worrying ordinarily benefits no one. It is rational thinking, not worrying and rumination, which can lead to a reasonable solution to a problem. Worrying and ruminating are themselves excess baggage that tend to obstruct your ability to solve problems.

Nor can the principle of respect for persons be used to defend your dutiful worrying. In fact, this principle would tell you to avoid engaging in it. This is because in engaging in dutiful worrying, you are treating yourself as a mere means, that is, as an object whose worth or value is exhausted by whether or not you solve your problems. Worrying takes away your personal autonomy by demanding that you set aside your own desires and dreams for the sake of finding that illusive perfect solution.

But what if you are the object of your dutiful-worrying concerns? Perhaps you have told yourself that you can't be happy unless you find the perfect mate. This means putting your happiness on hold until this person is located (which will be never since no one is perfect). Again, your dutiful worrying has turned you into an accessory or tool, or a means to an end, which contradicts the principle of respect for persons.

Well then, maybe your dutiful worrying can be defended using care-based ethics. After all, when you worry yourself sick about your loved ones, are you not demonstrating profound caring for the ones you love?

Clearly, you are trying to prevent the suffering of your loved ones. But there is more to care-based ethics than this. First, this approach to morality stresses the preservation of interpersonal relationships, and the caring you do as a dutiful worrier creates and exacerbates nervous tension that works against the preservation of interpersonal relationships. Second, as you have seen, when you engage in dutiful worrying, you lose your perspective and objectivity by getting too close to the situation. In so doing, you lose your ability to make rational decisions.

Third, dutiful worrying is perfectionistic whereas care-based ethics is realistic. That is, while you may hope that everyone's interests are harmonized and no one ever gets hurt, care-based ethics does not require that a perfect outcome be attained and acknowledges the difficulty of attaining all-around satisfaction (Gilligan 1993). So while both dutiful worrying and the care-based approach prescribe aiming at a perfect outcome, only dutiful worrying demands that this outcome be realized, and as a result, it generates needless stress, which in turn defeats the very point of caring in the first place.

Therefore, not one of the three principle approaches to ethics justifies your dutiful worrying. To the contrary, according to each of these approaches, dutiful worrying should be avoided.

Clearly you are concerned about acting morally. It is what has led to your becoming a dutiful worrier in the first place. You have felt guilty when you tried not to worry because you think that you have a moral duty to worry and that you would be violating this duty if you didn't worry. However, it should now be obvious that worrying is not your duty. No legitimate approach to morality sanctions any such duty. In fact, the three main approaches to moral decision-making that you have just learned would tell you to stop your dutiful worrying and let yourself be happy.

There is a rational alternative to worrying, of course, and that is to use these three principles to make moral decisions and act on them. The rest of this chapter, along with chapter 10, will help you do that.

Be Prepared to Balance Competing Ethical Interests

In an ideal world, it might be possible to make decisions that are always beneficent, respectful, and caring. Unfortunately, in the real world this is not always possible, so you should be prepared for the possibility of conflict among these moral standards. What is respectful might not be beneficent, for example. In a medical context, a patient might refuse a needed therapy, even one that could save his life. Plainly, it would violate the principle of respect for persons to strap the patient down and perform the medical intervention, even though the patient might otherwise die.

Similarly, you might know that your adult child is doing something that he or she will probably come to regret. While you can justly admonish your child not to do it, ordinarily you cannot justly force or compel your child to listen to you. So you should be prepared to accept the fact that moral decision-making may require weighing competing ethical interests against each other.

There are also times when the right thing to do might not be care-based. Thus there are some interpersonal relations not worth preserving. If you are a survivor of domestic violence or sexual abuse, then you may have already come to appreciate this point. In cases of child abuse, the principle of respect for persons may conflict with the care-based interest in keeping the family intact, for trying to preserve the family would be to treat the children as a mere means to this end. In caring for the child, it may be necessary to remove her from the home, and in the most egregious cases of abuse, the right thing may be to seek criminal charges against a parent.

Reframe Your Moral Rules to Allow for Exceptions

Moral standards may conflict because they are not absolute, that is, they are not unconditional. However, if you are like most people, you were probably taught that you should always tell the truth and never lie; that you should always keep your promises; that you should never injure or kill another human being; that you should never steal.

Such unconditional moral rules as these are unrealistic. Indeed, in this imperfect world, lying may be sometimes justified; some promises should be broken; some cases of injuring or killing another, as in self-defense, are excusable; and stealing something, if it means saving a life, can be morally acceptable.

Sometimes telling the truth or keeping a promise may conflict with not bringing on harm, and sometimes telling a lie may even save a life. Dutiful worriers invest themselves in trying to bring perfect order to a world that is not as tidy as they want it to be. Coming to see this point can save you hours of worrying and rumination: *Okay, I hate to have to break my promise to my child. He was so much counting on getting that new toy I promised to buy him. But I know now that it is made with toxic chemicals, and I can no longer honor my promise.* Instead of trying to make a square peg fit into a round hole, you can, with the exercise of such rational discretion, short-circuit hours of wasteful rumination.

Allowing for exceptions to the rule does not mean giving up on such moral rules as those against breaking promises, lying, harming others, and so forth. However, dropping the use of terms like "always" and "never," as in "It is always wrong to break promises" or "You should never tell a lie," will help you make more rational moral decisions. For example, you might modify these statements to say that "Lying tends to be wrong" and "Promise-breaking tends to be wrong." If you allow for exceptions, you will be less likely to feel guilty if you choose to break a promise or tell a lie under exceptional circumstances. For in such cases, these acts may not even be morally wrong.

Be Prepared to Tolerate Ambiguity

Because moral standards and rules are not unconditional, you will need to rely on your discretion in weighing and balancing competing ethical interests in particular situations. In other words, there is an inherent ambiguity to moral decision-making. As Aristotle long ago made clear, ethics is not math. There are general guidelines, but there are no formulas or algorithms. Moral decision-making can indeed be a messy business, which is one reason why such decision-making is so hard for dutiful worriers. In accepting such inherent ambiguity, however, you can combat your dutiful perfectionism and attain greater serenity.

If you wait to be certain about what to do, you could be waiting forever. Moral standards and rules can take you just so far, and the rest relies on your willingness to make a decision.

◆ French Resistance

The French thinker Jean-Paul Sartre (2000) gives this instructive example. During the Nazi occupation of France, a student of his came to see him for moral advice. The student was torn between joining the resistance forces to fight the Nazis and staying home with his mother. The Nazis had killed this student's brother, and he wanted to avenge his brother's death. On the other hand, his mother didn't want him to enlist, and he knew how hard this would be on her, since she had already lost her other son.

Nor were there any guarantees, no matter what he decided to do. If he enlisted, he could possibly get stuck at a desk job and not see any military action, thus defeating his point for joining in the first place. On the other hand, if he stayed home, he would satisfy his mother but then miss the chance to fight the Nazis.

No ethical standard could provide an unambiguous answer to the student's question. So what did Sartre ultimately advise? Make a decision, said Sartre, for ultimately it is the act of deciding that makes the decision right. If the student felt strongly enough about enlisting, then that would be the right thing for him to do. If he felt that satisfying his mother's wishes was more important, then staying home would be the right thing for him to do. Indeed, this student could have procrastinated about the decision until he had finally made his decision by indecision. Instead, he simply had to make a decision and run with it.

While not all moral choices need be so ambiguous, you should be prepared to encounter some ambiguity in making your own moral choices. You cannot expect that the facts of a situation will fit neatly under unconditional moral standards or rules, and you will often need to exercise discretion. This is a fact of moral life. Holding out for the perfect solution to a moral choice is likely to keep you in a perpetual state of needless stress. Notwithstanding the inherent ambiguity of moral choices, you should exercise your willpower to stop your procrastination, make your decision, and act on it.

Be Prepared to Have Regrets

Making a rational moral decision does not mean that you will have no regrets after making it. Most people will feel some regret even if they believe they have done the right thing. This is especially true if the decision was difficult. Consider the case of Marcy.

• Marcy's Story

Marcy was recently widowed. Her husband, John, had been in a car accident and, as a result, was in a persistent vegetative state for about one year. Due to extensive damage to his cerebral cortex, it was highly unlikely that John would ever regain consciousness. His lower brain stem was functional, however, and he did not require a respirator. He had a feeding tube implanted into his abdomen so that he could receive adequate nutrition.

While John did not have a living will, Marcy and John had previously discussed end-of-life decisions with each other, and it was clear what John's wishes would be. He had told Marcy that he would not want to be maintained in a vegetative state past one year if there were no reasonable possibility for a return to a rational existence.

John had been a physics professor who had lectured throughout the world. On many occasions, he had told Marcy that he valued his ability to think and reason above all else and that his life would be pointless if it were prolonged in a vegetative state.

The decision weighed heavily on Marcy. Even though John was nonresponsive, it was difficult for her to accept the finality of ending his biological existence. She would no longer be able to visit him. All hope would come to a resounding end. A vacant feeling welled up inside her every time she entertained the idea of ending his life. However, she was aware that sustaining him past one year would not be what he would have wanted and that she would therefore be imposing her own wishes on him. So Marcy decided to have the feeding tube removed, and within a week, John passed away.

In the end, Marcy realized that she had made a rational decision. There was no significant possibility of John's returning to a meaningful existence. John was clear about his wishes in these tragic circumstances. The decision was also consistent with the high premium he had set on rationality as a condition of meaningful life. Marcy had waited a full year. Sustaining him in a persistent vegetative state past a year would have catered only to her refusal to let go.

Still, Marcy had regrets. She wondered whether waiting longer could have made any difference. She would have been willing to wait longer had John not been so clear about his wishes and even though waiting longer probably would have made no difference. She regretted having to be the one to give the consent to end John's life. Yet despite these regrets, she felt that she had done the right thing.

Life inevitably involves tradeoffs. Sometimes we have to make tough choices, and sometimes they will be accompanied by regret. Having such regrets is an unavoidable part of living.

The Final Step

This chapter has given you some important guidelines for making more rational moral choices. These guidelines will be useful as you begin to think proactively about your problems, make rational moral decisions, and use your willpower muscle to stop worrying and act on your decision. This final step of exercising your willpower to act instead of worrying will be covered in chapter 10.

CHAPTER 10

Acting Instead of Worrying

Much of moral decision-making is about being proactive. This chapter will focus on *proactive thinking*, which means thinking about how to solve problems rather than worrying about them. It is the sort of thinking that tends to lead to action. Accordingly, this chapter offers a user-friendly method for making and implementing proactive moral decisions. This will, in turn, help you take the final step in the four-step program for overcoming dutiful worrying: using your willpower to stop worrying.

Dilemma Thinking Vs. Proactive Thinking

When people worry excessively about their problems, they tend to turn them into dilemmas. As discussed in chapter 8, dilemma thinking is thinking in which you conceive of your situation as that of choosing between two options both of which have undesirable consequences: *I'm damned if I do and damned if I don't!* So, vacillating between the undesirable horns of your dilemma, you can end up staying where you're at and making your decision by indecision. Through such indecision, you lose the opportunity to make a choice based on evidence and rational thinking.

This is not to say that you can always easily avoid seeing some situations as dilemmas. There are, after all, some true dilemmas. For example, we may face such an unavoidable dilemma in wrestling with a disease when the only available treatment may be as risky as the disease itself. Yet many dilemmas that people frame are artificially conceived and need not be presented as dilemmas in the first place. In such cases, you should avoid dilemma thinking altogether.

Proactive thinking, unlike dilemma thinking, leads you to a conclusion about what to do rather than keeping you ruminating about how you are caught between a rock and a hard place. Thus, instead of vacillating between the undesirable consequences of staying at your present job or looking for another one, you could weigh the potential benefits as well as the potential costs of each option and choose the option that on balance appears to be better. This would be proactive thinking because it applies a method for making a decision.

It's easy enough to create a dilemma about almost anything if you are looking for the drawbacks of whatever you do and then allow yourself to stew on them. One key to avoiding such decision by indecision, however, is to avoid creating dilemmas in the first place: *So I should stop hanging myself up on damned-if-I-do and damned-if-I-don't thinking and look instead for solutions to the problems I have.*

Five Steps to Thinking Proactively

Proactive thinking is methodical thinking and therefore proceeds in terms of a series of general steps. There are five principal steps. First, define your problem. Second, gather morally relevant facts. Third, think of some possible solutions to your problem. Fourth, choose the solution that you think is, on balance, the most beneficent, respectful, and caring. Fifth, implement your decision. Here's a look at each of these steps in turn.

Step 1: Defining Your Problem

To think proactively, the first thing to do is to define your problem. Here it is important to keep in mind that you have a moral problem when there is a good chance that what you do can significantly affect the welfare, interests, or needs of someone or other. The seriousness of your problem will depend on what these effects are and how probable they are. Indeed, if what you do has a high probability of determining whether a person lives or dies (many physicians make such decisions regularly), then you have a serious moral problem. If what you do has a slight chance of, say, disappointing someone, then your problem would be relatively minor. Unfortunately, many dutiful worriers tend to catastrophize and worry about even such relatively minor problems, which can place undue stress on them and others.

To define your moral problem, you need to ask a question that you want answered, which, depending on how it's answered, may have significant consequences for the welfare, interests, or needs of someone or other. Here, *welfare* includes positive welfare (benefit) and negative welfare (harm), including both physical and mental types of benefit and harm, for example, physical as well as emotional pain and suffering. *Interests* include people's goals, such as career or educational goals, and also basic human rights, such as the right to privacy, free speech, religious freedom, and the right to informed consent in healthcare. *Needs* include physical conditions essential or important to survival, such as food and water, clothing, and shelter, but may also be understood to include common human desires, such as for sex, love, and friendship.

An example of a moral problem would be the question, should you tell your elderly mother the truth that she has terminal cancer? Indeed, this question defines a serious moral problem, because what you do is likely to significantly affect the welfare, interests, or needs of your mother. Thus, your mother has an interest in knowing the truth because she may wish to get her affairs in order before she dies. According to the principle of respect for persons, she would also have a right to know the truth, for in keeping the truth from her you would be manipulating her like an object. On the other hand, if you tell her about her cancer, there is a possibility she may become depressed and spend the remaining days of her life in such a state.

Moral problems can also concern your own welfare, interests, or needs. For example, suppose your question is whether you should agree to live with your boyfriend. Since the answer to this question can have a chance of significantly affecting your future happiness (as well as that of your boyfriend), it defines a moral problem.

Accordingly, you should start your moral inquiries with questions, not answers. Answers come later. This is a departure from dilemma thinking, which begins with statements about options and their bad consequences and leads to a conclusion about how, no matter what you do, something bad will happen. But such a conclusion is unproductive. In contrast, the conclusion to proactive thinking is always an answer to a question, and this can be productive.

The question you raise should also be open ended. That is, it should not assume any answers to questions you have not already examined. For example, if you ask, "How can I convince my boyfriend to live with me?" you are assuming that you should try to convince him to live with you. But maybe he isn't ready to take the relationship to this level. Moreover, you are also assuming that living together is the best thing for your relationship, but perhaps you have not carefully thought this through. A less question-begging question might therefore be "Should I discuss with my boyfriend the issue of living together?" In contrast to the first formulation, this second question has the virtue of being respectful of potential differences about cohabitation before marriage. So, in raising your problem-defining questions, you should be careful to avoid assuming that you already know the answers to any important questions that you haven't yet asked.

EXERCISE: Define Your Moral Problem

Think for a moment about a moral problem you have that you would like to address. Now, take out your pen or pencil and write down a question that defines your moral problem. Remember, this question must be one you want answered, and it must define a moral problem; that is, how you answer it will have a good chance of significantly affecting the welfare, interests, or needs of someone or other. Moreover, remember that your questions shouldn't assume an answer to some other question that you haven't yet already addressed.

Now make a list of how you think your response to this question could affect the welfare, interests, or needs of different parties, including yourself if appropriate. Note that your list could have several entries or even one, depending on the number of *stakeholders*, or how many people you think might be affected by your decision.

Step Two: Gathering Morally Relevant Facts

Once you have defined your moral problem, your next step will be to gather morally relevant facts. A *morally relevant fact* is a fact that is relevant to the welfare, interests, or needs of the different parties at stake. For example, some statistics regarding the percentage of successful relationships with cohabitation prior to marriage would be morally relevant to the problem of whether to live with your boyfriend if you and your boyfriend have an interest in forging a successful relationship. Or, for example, your knowledge of how your mother has been able to handle bad news in the past would be morally relevant to your problem of whether to tell her that she has terminal cancer. Here your mother's ability to handle bad news is a major welfare concern and is therefore morally relevant to the problem at hand.

The past history of people, their desires, goals, beliefs, and even political and religious views could be morally relevant to a moral problem. Morally relevant facts might include physical facts like a person's health, her mental competence (or lack thereof), age, and ability to comprehend information. For example, if your mother were mentally incompetent, then this fact could have bearing on how much information she might be told about her illness or if you tell her anything about it. Or, for example, the religious convictions of a patient who happens to be a Jehovah's Witness could be morally relevant to a physician's question of whether to honor the patient's refusal of a life-saving blood transfusion. This is because the Jehovah's Witness faith interprets blood transfusions to be a transgression of a passage in the Old Testament about consumption of blood. Thus, if the physician refused to honor this patient's refusal of the blood transfusion, he would be violating her right to freedom of religious practice, which is both a basic moral right and a basic legal right.

Obviously, there are limits to what you can know, and you should not demand that your knowledge be perfect or that you have gathered every morally relevant fact. Indeed, gathering these facts could be an endless process, which would stifle decision-making and lead to inaction. While there is no formula for when to stop trying to find morally relevant facts, you can have a reasonable idea.

At the stage of asking your problem-defining question, you are likely to have a rather unclear idea of who the key stakeholders are and how they might be affected by your own actions. However, at a certain point in the fact-gathering process, you will start to get a reasonably clear (but not perfect) picture of who the key stakeholders are and how they might be affected by what you decide to do. For example, when the physician acquires the facts that his patient is a Jehovah's Witness, that this faith rejects blood transfusions, and that the patient or his or her legal guardian has competently refused such therapy, then the physician should have a reasonably clear picture of the stakes and the significance of alternative courses of action.

EXERCISE: Gather the Morally Relevant Facts

Take out your pen or pencil and make a list of facts that are morally relevant to the moral problem-defining question you articulated in the previous exercise. Remember that a morally relevant fact is a fact that is relevant to the welfare, interests, or needs of the different parties at stake. How many facts should you list? Try brainstorming for about five or ten minutes and see what you can come up with. Note too that at this stage you might become aware of other welfare, interests, or needs of which you were previously unaware. If this happens, feel free to add to the list that you generated in the previous exercise, where you defined your moral problem.

Has your list of morally relevant facts given you any new ideas or perspectives on your problem? If so, briefly jot down your new insights.

Step 3: Thinking of Possible Solutions

The gathering of morally relevant facts leads to the next step of coming up with some ideas about what you should do. For example, suppose you know that your mother has usually in the past been quite rational in receiving bad news. Moreover, you are aware that she places a high value on honesty and has always expected others to treat her with the same respect with which she treats others. Further, you know that she is a very responsible person and may want to get her affairs in order. Thus, not telling her that she has terminal cancer may prevent her from accomplishing one of her important goals. You also know that she is a religious person and may have religious interests that would be stifled by not telling her that she has terminal cancer. For example, she may be denied the opportunity to make suitable arrangements for her burial.

So, one possible solution is to tell her the truth now; another is to wait a little while longer before telling her. Another possible solution is not to tell her at all. However, in light of the facts, it may appear that the third possible solution (not telling her at all) would be less worthy than the other possible solutions, since it would appear to run counter to the welfare, interests, or needs of your mother that you have identified and clarified in the previous steps of the decision-making process.

EXERCISE: Think of Some Possible Solutions to Your Problem

Review the list of welfare, interests, or needs and the list of morally relevant facts you have generated in the previous exercises. In light of your lists, write down some possible solutions to your problem that you think are worthy of further consideration.

Step 4: Choosing the Most Beneficent, Respectful, and Caring Solution

After selecting some possible solutions for further consideration, you will then need to apply the three moral standards discussed in chapter 9: the principle of respect for persons, the principle of beneficence, and care-based ethics. You should ask yourself which of your possible solutions is, on balance, the most beneficent, respectful, and caring. In answering this question, you will reach a decision about what to do.

For example, if you told your mom now rather than later that she had terminal cancer, your decision would benefit her by allowing her to get her affairs in order and would give her maximal time to do so; it would also respect her right to be treated as a rational, self-determining person and therefore be respectful; and it would also be caring insofar as you would be using empathy to imagine how betrayed she would feel if you kept this information from her and perhaps how you would feel if the same thing were done to you. On the other hand, telling her later would buy her more time to live without having to face the painful awareness of her imminent demise. But there would be a price for this additional time. She would have less time to get her affairs in order, to work through and come to grips with the ultimate fact, and to make her peace with God. She would have to deal with the fact that this information was withheld from her, even if only temporarily. This would seem to work against the principle of respect for persons inasmuch as your mom has a right to her own healthcare information and records. There is also a question about how caring your withholding of the information would be. On the one hand, your motivation would be to give her more time to avoid having to deal with this grave truth. On the other hand, you have reason to think she would want to know as soon as possible, so withholding the information, even temporarily, would be against her wishes. Just how caring would it be to go against her wishes in this way? How would you feel if someone took it upon themselves to withhold information from you that you would have wanted to know?

So, on balance, it may appear that telling your mom now that she had terminal cancer would be the most beneficent, respectful, and caring thing to do. However, this need not be your decision. There may be alternative perspectives about the weighing and balancing of your moral standards.

For example, you might think that telling your mom later would provide a sort of mean between the excesses of telling her now and not telling her at all. You might think that the price of buying the extra time for her to live happily is indeed worth the sacrifice of respect for her right to know. You might thus conclude that waiting a while to tell her would, on balance, be the more beneficent, respectful, and caring thing to do.

When your moral standards take you in opposing directions or fail to give you an unambiguous answer, there is little else you can do but make a choice and stick with it. In these circumstances, which will not be infrequent, you will simply need to choose. Otherwise, you will not answer the problem-defining question you have posed to yourself. Proactive thinking calls for you to make a choice.

The ambiguity of moral decision-making notwithstanding, there is also rationality. You will have defined your problem, collected morally relevant facts, selected solutions that are worthy of consideration; and, according to a reasonable interpretation guided by rational standards of moral decision-making, you will have made a choice. Thus, you are not unlike a scientist who starts with a clearly defined problem, does her field work, advances alternative hypotheses, tests them, and selects the one that she thinks has the greatest predictive and explanatory power. You will have done your level best to make a rational moral decision in a world that does not give you a litmus test for morality. This is much better than procrastinating and never making any decision.

It won't be perfect. Thus, if you made a decision to tell your mother that she had terminal cancer, it would still be difficult for her to receive the tragic news, and you might regret having to be the one to tell her. But in this less than ideal world, you cannot expect to walk away from tough moral decisions without any regrets, even if you believe that your decisions have been rational.

EXERCISE: Make Your Moral Decision

Take about five minutes to contemplate the different solutions that you wrote down in the previous exercise and choose the one that you think, on balance, is the most beneficent, respectful, and caring.

Write down the solution you've chosen and next to it write, "This is what I have decided to do." Don't second-guess yourself. Once you have written down your solution to your moral problem, don't change it.

Step 5: Implementing Your Decision

The final step of proactive thinking is to act upon your decision. This means not simply coming to a conclusion but also putting it into action. This is where you will need to exercise willpower and not put off what you believe you should do.

Oftentimes, people make excuses: *Now is not the right time. I better wait until tomorrow to tell her.* Of course, tomorrow will be no less difficult than today to deliver the bad news. Thus, you may need to force yourself to do what you have decided to do.

I know how difficult this sort of thing can be. Morally right action is often considerably harder and more challenging to implement than morally irresponsible action. In the long run, however, you are more likely to feel better about having acted responsibly than having put off or neglected to implement a rational decision. So I hope you will exercise your willpower to carry through on what you have decided.

Formulating Your Behavioral Plan

To avoid the "I'll do it tomorrow" excuse, you will need to formulate a behavioral plan to specify the details of when, where, and how you're going to implement your solution. This plan should be detailed enough for you to carry out your decision but not so detailed that you get hung up in its formulation.

Today, after work, I am going to visit my mom. I am going to drop by at 6:00 p.m. after she has eaten dinner. I'm going to tell her that there's something important I need to speak to her about. We'll sit down in the living room together on the sofa where it's comfortable. I'm going to tell her that the MRI she took showed that she has a cancer that has spread throughout her body. I will tell her that the doctor said that the disease is too advanced to treat and that, although it is difficult to say, she could have four months. I'll suggest to her that we make an appointment to speak to the doctor.

With such a plan in place, you could then make yourself carry through with your decision. No longer are there the vagaries of when, where, and how. The plan is clear enough about these details, and the next step is also clear: to implement your decision according to plan.

EXERCISE: Formulate Your Behavioral Plan

Take a few minutes to write down a behavioral plan to implement the moral decision that you made in the last exercise. Include in your plan:

1. When you're going to implement your decision.

2. Where you're going to implement it.

3. How you're going to go about implementing it.

Remember, your plan doesn't have to be elaborate but rather needs to be a reasonable guide for how to act on your decision.

After you have formulated your plan, keep yourself from second-guessing it. In other words, don't change or revise it.

Exercising Your Willpower

Arriving at a moral decision is meaningless unless you act on it. Here you will need to take responsibility. You may fear that your plan of action could backfire and you would be a bad person for messing up. But you will need to exercise courage and self-respect and not demand perfection.

The interim period between making a decision and acting on it may be a time when you find yourself especially vulnerable to rumination and worrying. After all, you are used to doing this. So distract yourself with a behavioral assignment to do something you like to do, and exercise your willpower to make yourself do it. Speak rationally to yourself if you start to feel guilty: *Okay, it's possible that my plan can backfire and my mom will go into a deep, dark depression. But I can't predict the future perfectly. I have to live by probabilities. I'm also a person, not an object, so my self-worth doesn't depend on whether my plan works. I hope it works. I have good reason to think it's a reasonable solution. But I need to be prepared to tolerate disappointment too. I also know that I may have regrets. That's just part of making a moral choice.*

Nowhere is it written that you have a duty to worry and upset yourself. That's not part of the plan.

EXERCISE: Act on Your Behavioral Plan

Assuming that you have a window of time before carrying out the plan you formulated in the last exercise, give yourself a behavioral assignment to do something you enjoy doing. Make yourself do this activity even if you feel disinclined to do it.

When the time to act arrives, carry out your plan to implement your moral decision. Don't procrastinate, but stay on schedule and get the job done!

If you have worked through the exercises in this book, then you have had a number of opportunities to work on strengthening your willpower muscle. This is something that you will continue to need to do over the course of your life. It is not something you can postpone and forget about. As with any other muscle, you can either use it or lose it. And using it will make you more proficient at stopping your worrying.

Indeed, willpower is what makes human beings free. Without it, we would be unable to stop ourselves from having irrational emotions and acting on them whenever we have them. As a dutiful worrier, you have allowed fear and other emotions to get the better of you. But you can, with practice, set yourself free.

CHAPTER 11

How to Stop Worrying Without Feeling Guilty

This book has provided you with some valuable tools for overcoming your habit of dutiful worrying and becoming a proactive thinker. You should be well on your way to greatly reducing the needless stress that worry has brought to your life.

Each chapter of this book has concentrated on a different aspect of the four-step program. Collectively, they fit together to form a powerful, systematic cognitive behavioral approach to overcoming dutiful worrying. Here is a summary of this systematic approach:

The Four-Step Program for Overcoming Your Dutiful Worrying

Step 1. Identify your faulty reasoning. Use your dutiful-worrying template (chapter 3).

Step 2. Refute your reasoning fallacies (losing-control anxiety, self-damnation, and dutiful perfectionism). Use your refutation check-lists (chapter 4).

Step 3. Take a rational perspective: Select and apply your cognitive antidotes to each reasoning fallacy (chapters 6, 7, and 8). Review your guidelines for making moral decisions (chapter 9). Think pro-actively about your problem (chapter 10). Give yourself at least one behavioral assignment to do something you enjoy (chapter 2).

Step 4. Use your willpower to stop worrying: Remind yourself of the fallacies in your dutiful-worrying reasoning (chapter 4). Enforce your cognitive antidotes by applying them to your present situation (chapters 6, 7 and 8). Do your behavioral assignment or assignments to do something you enjoy (chapter 10). Implement your behavioral plan (chapter 10).

Proficiency in overcoming your worrying will take practice, and you may find that you need further practice with some aspects of the program more than others. You may have found that a discussion in one chapter or another seemed to speak more directly to your issues. This knowledge may guide you as you continue to work on overcoming your dutiful worrying.

Luckily, this four-step program is flexible, so you can focus on whichever virtues you want to continue to strengthen and choose the antidotes to dutiful worrying that work best for you. For example, you may have perceived that you have a larger problem with losing-control anxiety than with self-damnation. If this is the case, you may be more inclined to work further on building courage than on building unconditional self-respect. Or you may be more interested in cultivating serenity to overcome your dutiful perfectionism than you are in developing other virtues.

This said, I should add that in my experience in working with dutiful worriers, most people benefit from the practice of refuting and finding antidotes to losing-control anxiety, self-damnation, and demanding perfection, even if they feel that they tend to make one of these reasoning fallacies more than another. So, it's a good idea to go through all the steps of the program whenever you find yourself ruminating and worrying rather than thinking proactively about a moral problem. The more familiar you become with this new kind of thinking and behaving, the more automatic it will become.

Stop Feeling Guilty

One of the biggest challenges you will have in overcoming your dutiful worrying is to avoid caving in to the guilty feelings you may have when you try not to worry. Even though you now are aware that continuing to worry is irrational, you may still feel guilty when you don't. This is because there is a difference between intellectually appreciating that you are thinking or behaving irrationally and emotionally appreciating it. Psychologists refer to this disparity between intellectual and emotional appreciation as *cognitive dissonance*.

Please don't feel discouraged if you find yourself in a state of cognitive dissonance. It can actually be a good thing because it means that you can recognize when you are thinking or behaving irrationally, and this is a sign that you are in a position to change. Your challenge is to bring your emotional appreciation in line with your intellectual appreciation of the fact that dutiful worrying is irrational. Indeed, you are now on route to cultivating the skills that can help you accomplish this.

So how can you overcome your cognitive dissonance and thereby stop feeling guilty? The key is to practice your new skills whenever you start to feel guilty. You now have access to your dutiful-worrying reasoning. You have precise knowledge as to where its fallacies are located, what these fallacies are, and how to refute them; how to construct rational antidotes to overcome them; how to make moral decisions and construct a behavioral plan to implement your decisions; what behavioral assignments to give yourself to keep you from ruminating needlessly about your problem; and how to act on your behavioral plan.

If you are willing to work at applying these skills, then you can stop yourself from feeling guilty. You can decide to stop feeling guilty by recognizing that all this worrying has wasted enough valuable time and produced enough needless stress. You can decide that this stress is unhealthy (physically as well as psychologically) for you and those about whom you care so much. You can decide to put your four-step program into action and to keep it up.

I urge you not to give in to your guilt. Dutiful worrying is a habit, and habits tend to grow stronger over time unless you do something to try to change them. They continue to get stronger and stronger, the more you persist in a particular pattern of thinking, feeling, and behaving. The more you engage in dutiful worrying, the more you will be inclined to engage in it. On the other hand, this can work in reverse. The more success you have in stopping your worrying and not feeling guilty about it, the better you will get at doing this.

For the dutiful worrier who has not acquired the cognitive behavioral skills addressed in this book, worrying will seem like the moral thing to do, and because it will seem like the moral thing to do, the dutiful worrier will feel guilty if she tries not to worry: *How could I not worry? I have to worry. What kind of person would I be if I didn't worry! Wouldn't you worry too if you thought that you were doing something morally wrong if you didn't worry?*

However, you have seen that such worrying is not a moral duty and never was. No legitimate moral standard supports dutiful worrying, for it is not beneficent, respectful, or caring. In fact, far from justifying dutiful worrying, every moral standard would argue against it.

Dutiful worrying causes needless stress and, as a result, adversely affects your rational ability to solve problems. In engaging in it, you treat yourself like an object and fail to respect your inherent value as a human person. Far from cultivating and preserving interpersonal relationships, it hampers them by injecting needless stress into them.

So is it right for you to feel guilty about refusing to engage in an activity that has such deleterious effects on human happiness? The answer to this question can only be a resounding no!

Then stop worrying and please, please don't feel guilty about it. This is in your power, and you now have the tools at your disposal to succeed. You can do it. You really should.

References

Aristotle. 1941. *Nicomachean ethics.* In *The Basic Works of Aristotle*, edited by Richard McKeon. New York: Random House

Bandura, Albert. 1990. Mechanisms of moral disengagement in terrorism. In *Origins of Terrorism: Psychologies, Ideologies, Theologies, States of Mind*, edited by W. Reich. Cambridge: Cambridge University Press.

Beauchamp, Tom, and James Childress. 2008. *Principles of Biomedical Ethics.* New York: Oxford University Press.

Copi, Irving, and Carl Cohen. 1998. *Introduction to Logic.* 10th ed. Upper Saddle River, NJ: Prentice-Hall.

Ellis, Albert. 1999. *How to Make Yourself Happy and Remarkably Less Disturbable.* Atascadero, CA: Impact Books.

Epictetus. 2009. *The Discourses*, translated by George Long. The Internet Classics Archive. http://classics.mit.edu//Epictetus/discourses.html (accessed June 2, 2010).

Epicurus. 2003. Letter to Menoeceus, translated by Russel M. Geer. In *From Plato to Derrida*, edited by Forrest E. Baird and Walter Kaufmann. 4th ed. Upper Saddle River, N.J.: Prentice-Hall.

Frankl, Vicktor. 1984. *Man's Search for Meaning: An Introduction to Logotherapy.* New York: Simon and Schuster. (This translation by Ilse Lasch first published by Beacon Press in 1959).

Gilligan, Carol. 1993. *In a Different Voice: Psychological Theory and Women's Development.* Cambridge, MA: Harvard University Press.

Hume, David. 2003. Enquiry concerning human understanding. In *From Plato to Derrida*, edited by Forrest E. Baird and Walter Kaufmann. 4th ed. Upper Saddle River, N.J.: Prentice Hall.

James, William. 1995. *Pragmatism.* New York: Dover.

Kant, Immanuel. 1964. *Groundwork of the Metaphysics of Morals*, translated by H. J. Paton. New York: Harper and Row.

Nietzsche, Friedrich. 1954. *Beyond good and evil*, translated by Helen Zimmern. In *The Philosophy of Nietzsche.* New York: Random House.

Rieder, Michael J. 1994. Mechanisms of unpredictable adverse drug reactions. *Drug Safety* 11 (3): 196–212.

Rogers, Carl. 1961. *On Becoming a Person.* Boston: Houghton Mifflin.

Sartre, Jean-Paul. 2000. *Existentialism*, translated by Bernard Frechman. In *Philosophers at Work: Issues and Practice of Philosophy*, edited by Elliot D. Cohen. Fort Worth, TX: Harcourt.

Van der Leeuw, J. J. 2003. *The Conquest of Illusion.* Whitefish, MT: Kessinger Publishing.

Elliot D. Cohen, PhD, is professor and chair of the department of humanities at Indian River State College, adjunct professor of clinical ethics at the Florida State University College of Medicine, and director of the Institute of Critical Thinking. The author of numerous books and articles, he is a principal founder of philosophical counseling in the United States and inventor of logic-based therapy. He writes a blog for *Psychology Today* and has been quoted in major media venues, including *New York Times Magazine*.

more books from newharbingerpublications, inc.

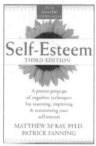

WOMEN WHO WORRY TOO MUCH

How to Stop Worry & Anxiety from Ruining Relationships, Work & Fun

US $16.95 / ISBN: 97

SELF-ESTEEM, THIRD EDITION

US $17.95 / ISBN: 978-1572241985
Also available as an **eBook**
at newharbinger.com

BUDDHA'S BRAIN

The Practical Neuroscience of Happiness, Love & Wisdom

US $17.95 / ISBN: 978-1572246959
Also available as an **eBook**
...binger.com

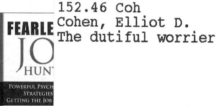

FEARLESS JOB HUNTING

Powerful Psychological Strategies for Getting the Job You Want

US $16.95 / ISBN: 978-1572248342
Also available as an **eBook**
at newharbinger.com

GET OUT OF YOUR MIND & INTO YOUR LIFE

The New Acceptance & Commitment Therapy

US $21.95 / ISBN: 978-1572244252
Also available as an eBook
at newharbinger.com

YOUR LIFE ON PURPOSE

How to Find What Matters & Create the Life You Want

US $16.95 / ISBN: 978-1572249059
Also available as an **eBook**
at newharbinger.com

available from

newharbingerpublications, inc.

& fine booksellers everywhere

To order, call toll free **1-800-748-6273**
or visit our online bookstore at **www.newharbinger.com**

(VISA, MC, AMEX / prices subject to change without notice)

Check out www.psychsolve.com

PsychSolve® offers help with diagnosis, including treatment information on mental health issues, such as depression, bipolar disorder, anxiety, phobias, stress & trauma, relationship problems, eating disorders, chronic pain, & many other disorders.